D1736383

MANAGEMENT ACCOUNTANT'S GUIDE TO FRAUD DISCOVERY AND CONTROL

THE WILEY/INSTITUTE OF MANAGEMENT ACCOUNTANTS
PROFESSIONAL BOOK SERIES

Denis W. Day • *How to Cut Business Travel Costs*

Harry L. Brown • *Design and Maintenance of Accounting Manuals*

Gordon V. Smith • *Corporate Valuation: A Business and Professional Guide*

Henry Labus • *Successfully Managing Your Accounting Career*

Ralph G. Loretta • *The Price Waterhouse Guide to Financial Management: Tools for Improving Performance*

James A. Brimson • *Activity Accounting: An Activity-Based Costing Approach*

Jack Fox • *Starting and Building Your Own Accounting Business, Second Edition*

Howard R. Davia, Patrick C. Coggins, John C. Wideman, and Joseph T. Kastantin • *Management Accountant's Guide to Fraud Discovery and Control*

MANAGEMENT ACCOUNTANT'S GUIDE TO FRAUD DISCOVERY AND CONTROL

HOWARD R. DAVIA
PATRICK C. COGGINS
JOHN C. WIDEMAN
JOSEPH T. KASTANTIN

JOHN WILEY & SONS, INC.

New York • Chichester • Brisbane • Toronto • Singapore

Library of Congress Cataloging-in-Publications Data:

Management accountant's guide to fraud discovery and control / Howard
R. Davia ... [et al.].

    p.   cm. — (The Wiley/Institute of Management Accountants
professional book series)

  Includes bibliographical references and index.

  ISBN 0-471-55595-9

  1. Auditing, Internal.   2. Managerial accounting.   3. Fraud.
I. Davia, Howard R., 1947–   . II. Series.
HF5668.25.M36   1992   91-32086
657'.458–dc20   CIP

Printed in the United States of America

10 9 8 7 6 5 4 3 2 1

ABOUT THE AUTHORS

Howard R. Davia is a former executive with both the U.S. General Accounting Office and the General Services Administration. He is a certified public accountant with over 30 years experience in government, industry, and public accounting. He has vast experience in the detection and deterrence of fraud. Mr. Davia is president and cofounder of Executive Education Series, Inc., which provides training and consulting in fraud discovery and control. The firm has been engaged in a joint venture with the College of Business Administration, University of Wisconsin–La Crosse for the purpose of conducting nationally the Fraud Discovery and Control Workshop. He is the principal author of the fraud auditing training material for this workshop and the Effective Fraud Auditing Workshop upon which the *Management Accountant's Guide to Fraud Discovery and Control* is based. Mr. Davia is an adjunct professor of accountancy at the University of Wisconsin–La Crosse.

Patrick C. Coggins is the Dupont Endowed Chair Professor at Stetson University and holds a J.D., and Ph.D. degrees in Administration and Adult Development and Education. He has over 20 years experience in the areas of governmental and public sector financial management, contract management, legal issues, organizational diagnosis, and income taxes. He has published books, articles, and papers nationally and has extensive lecturing and consulting experience. Professor Coggins is the author of Chapter 11, "Rules of Evidence."

John C. Wideman, Ph.D., has over 20 years experience in the civil, criminal, and intelligence fields as an investigator at the federal and state levels, and in private practice. He is a graduate of the FBI

National Academy, the Federal Law Enforcement Training Center, and the U.S. Army Intelligence Center and School. He has taught investigative courses for the U.S. government and several state agencies. Dr. Wideman is a practicing private investigator. He is the author of Chapter 10, "Investigating Suspected Fraud."

Joseph T. Kastantin is a consultant, author, and assistant professor of accountancy at the University of Wisconsin–La Crosse. Mr. Kastantin is both a certified public accountant and a certified management accountant. He earned a master's degree in business administration from Butler University, Indianapolis. He is the author of a book entitled *Professional Accounting Practice Management* (Quorum Books, 1988) and has authored and co-authored several articles on the topics of management, business control, and taxation. Mr. Kastantin is a co-founder of Executive Education Series, Inc.

FOREWORD

Fraud auditing is continuing to develop as an emerging profession. However, many significant issues continue to face professionals who wish to enhance their skills within this field. Resolution of these issues could ultimately dictate the validity of the entire profession.

Perhaps the single most predominant issue centers on the responsibility for detection and prevention of fraudulent activity. It has been estimated by the U.S. Chamber of Commerce that the impact of employee and management fraud exceeds $100 billion annually. In one way or another, fraudulent activity affects all of us as consumers, stockholders, or taxpayers. Professional fraud auditors must be given the background and support necessary to complete the task at hand.

Recent developments such as the *Report of the National Commission on Fraudulent Financial Reporting* (a.k.a. the Treadway Commission; Committee of Sponsoring Organizations of the Treadway Commission, New York, 1987), Congress's investigation of the accounting profession's role in fraudulent financial reporting, and the crisis in the savings and loan industry continue to reemphasize the significance and importance of needed redirection within the profession. The Committee of Sponsoring Organizations of the Treadway Commission issued an exposure draft on March 12, 1991, entitled *Internal Control—Integrated Framework*. This document is unique as it is jointly sponsored by several professional organizations that individually have varying interests in controlling fraud.

The dominant theme throughout much of the discussion appears to be that, in the future, the direction of fraud auditing must be proactive in nature. Today internal auditing is still dominated by conventional reactive audit thinking. A significant emphasis, or perhaps a majority of the emphasis, is placed on analyzing a problem after the damage has occurred. While there is merit in this process, a greater emphasis must be concentrated on helping management accountants focus on anticipating problems and limiting the consequences. This is what the *Management Accountant's Guide to Fraud Discovery and Control* is all about. Throughout the publication, the authors have taken a "hands on" approach and prepared material designed to improve auditors' backgrounds in investigative skills, as well as in issue and problem definition.

When fraud is involved, the internal auditor or independent CPA must frequently perform many of the same tasks as the private investigator. This includes following clues, investigating relationships, and obtaining information not available in financial records. In his text on corporate fraud (Bolonga, Jack G., *Corporate Fraud: The Basics of Prevention and Detection,* Butterworth, 1984), Bolonga indicates that the proper mindset is actually more important than methodology in fraud detection. He indicates that fraud detection is more an art than a science and requires innovative and creative thinking. The characteristics of persistence, doggedness, and self-confidence are needed to be an effective fraud auditor.

Business education programs have been criticized with the argument that traditional approaches to teaching accounting education (including internal auditing) have not developed students to their fullest learning potential. The Treadway Commission Report, for example, recommends that "accounting curricula should help students develop stronger analytical, problem-solving, and judgment skills to help prevent, detect and deter fraudulent financial reporting." We might add that the above-mentioned characteristics are valuable in the discovery of all types of fraudulent activity, not only fraudulent financial reporting. One might argue also that a major problem might be that under existing standards and regulations, accounting faculty have not been provided with sufficient guidelines to apply these recommendations to the instruction of fraud auditing. This text attempts to remedy that problem.

Additional evidence of the need for a greater emphasis on auditing for fraud is provided by a recent article in the *Internal Auditor* (Park, Theresa, "Fraud Findings: Business Fraud as Reported by Internal Auditors, *Internal Auditor*, June 1989). Theresa Park, its author, reviewed case histories of the "Fraud Findings" section of the journal over the past seven years. Analysis of how frauds were detected showed that 37% were discovered in the course of routine audits, 61% were discovered by accident, and the remaining 2% by other means. It is overwhelming to think that companies must rely on "accidental discovery" for detection of a majority of fraudulent activity.

The study further indicated that no industry is immune to fraud. This analysis showed that the largest number of fraud cases occurred in manufacturing companies and the second largest in governmental units. The author reported that, surprisingly, frauds against the U.S. government constituted about 10% of the overall total. However, this may indicate a strong need for greater fraud detection activity in this environment.

The greatest number of frauds were committed at the middle management level. Individuals at this level usually have authority to approve key transactions and possibly override specified internal controls. The fraudulent objective of middle managers was to deceive the company, whereas that of top managers was to deceive stockholders or parties outside the company.

Motivation and types of perpetrators varied—from disgruntled employees to those who wished to support expensive lifestyles to those with financial problems related to a family illness. There was no single most dominant reason for a fraudulent activity. However, control weaknesses, caused either by lack of internal control or failure to enforce existing internal control, were found to be prevalent.

In the area of actions taken against perpetrators, the study revealed that 77.5% of the organizations did not recover any funds. Of the 22.5% that recovered, 18.5% was from perpetrators and 4% from bonding companies. However, only 24% of the detected frauds led to prosecution and dismissal of an employee. Among the total number of frauds, only 8% resulted in conviction and 6% in actual incarceration. Professor Coggins, in Chapter 11, "Rules of Evidence," urges that this remarkably low prosecution rate be increased to the maximum rate possible as a deterrent to potential perpetrators of fraud.

The evidence is clear. Many organizations discover only a very small portion of ongoing fraudulent activity. Allowing this to continue undoubtedly results in significant costs to those organizations. The materials presented in this book are designed to close this

FOREWORD

floodgate of losses by increasing the auditor's sensitivity to fraud and improving the auditor's skills in discovering and controlling fraudulent activity.

RONALD R. BOTTIN, Ph.D.

Dean, College of Business Administration
Southwest Missouri State University
Springfield, Missouri

PREFACE

The authors undertook the task of writing the *Management Accountant's Guide to Fraud Discovery and Control* aware of certain existing factors that would influence the work and its reception in business world.

First, the *Management Accountant's Guide to Fraud Discovery and Control* is somewhat unique. There are many books on the topic of fraud and fraudulent financial reporting. There are also manuals prepared by various organizations that guide the auditor through an audit engagement, either internally or externally conducted. Off-the-shelf software is now available which purports to deter fraud.

The *Management Accountant's Guide to Fraud Discovery and Control* is designed to be a stand-alone reference. It is comprehensive in its coverage of fraud auditing, letting the auditor know what to do to deter potential perpetrators of fraud and what to do when indicia of fraud are found. Yet the authors also recognize that fraud auditing cannot be conducted effectively in an organization without the dedicated support of top management. Therefore great care has been taken to avoid, where possible, highly technical terms and details. They have done this to encourage wider distribution of this guide-book and to include the interests of individuals in top management regardless of their prior education and experience. The authors feel that if top management has an overall understanding of fraud auditing and its role in controlling their organizations, they will more readily support the fraud auditor's efforts.

The authors recognized that for this book to be accepted in the business world which is hyper-marketing-oriented, making the *Management Accountant's Guide to Fraud Discovery and Control* clearly different would be important. They have undertaken this task and trust that the business world will find it to be a useful and specialized tool for management accountants and progressive auditors who seek to undertake fraud-specific audits.

Second, there are no existing standards to guide the fraud auditor as there are for the independent accountant. Until such standards exist there will be continued reluctance in the accounting profession to engage in fraud-specific audits. Liability insurance carriers are extremely reluctant to insure auditing firms that engage in fraud-specific auditing. A separate fraud auditing service, performed in accordance with *generally accepted principles and standards* as proposed in Chapter 7, "Fraud Auditing Standards, Methodology, and Classifications", would surely encourage insurers to examine more objectively the risk that they would be asked to assume as liability insurance carriers for independent accountants offering those services.

In the interim, management accountants and internal auditors are the most likely candidates to engage in fraud auditing. They are on-site and have a firm grasp of the existing internal controls, their strengths, and their weaknesses. For these individuals to engage in fraud auditing they need a clear line of authority and commitment from top management. Additionally, they must be encouraged by management's seeing that the discoveries and disclosures they make are swiftly and visibly acted upon. In most cases this should result in prosecution of the perpetrator.

There are two separate types of fraud that are addressed in this book. Fraudulent financial reporting, which we refer to as "Treadway fraud," prompts the greatest investor and lender attention. Specific acts of transaction fraud not affecting financial reporting, however, are far more common and far more expensive than fraudulent financial reporting. Furthermore, the two types of fraud have different origins. Fraudulent financial reporting tends to be generated and practiced by top management and business owners in order to attract investor and lender capital. Middle management may also play the fraudulent reporting game by leading top management into believing that certain goals have been met or exceeded. Compensation tends to be tied to managerial performance. Therefore, middle management has a built-in incentive to make financial statements look as good as possible.

The Executive Education Series, Inc. is primarily interested in the second type of fraud, that is, specific fraudulent acts of individuals, otherwise known as white-collar crime. Fraud-specific auditing procedures are necessary for systematic discovery and control of fraud within an entity.

PREFACE

The *Management Accountant's Guide to Fraud Discovery and Control* is designed to serve as a detailed guide to persons interested in becoming competent in fraud auditing. This book may also be used as a valuable reference source for participants in the Effective Fraud Auditing workshop offered by the Professional Education Program of the Institute of Management Accountants, in Fraud Discovery and Control workshops, and in other programs on fraud offered by the Executive Education Series, Inc.

The art of fraud auditing has been privately developed by those few individuals around the world who have seen the need for fraud auditing skills. Therefore, much of the material in this book covers subject matter that has not previously been reduced to instructional form. It is the authors' intent that the *Management Accountant's Guide to Fraud Discovery and Control* will become the basis for the development of a separate field of specialization in fraud auditing.

The various chapters contain topics the authors believe to be essential to anyone wishing to become competent in fraud auditing. Two chapters draw heavily on previously developed materials. Chapter 10, "Investigating Suspected Fraud," is based on a variety of resources cited in the Bibliography. Chapter 11, "Rules of Evidence" is of necessity based on the common law and the United States Code.

The general public is somewhat myopic when it comes to fraud. In fact, in a recent interview on the Business Radio Network two of the authors were disappointed to find that most of the listener questions concerned consumer fraud, an altogether different subject. The public perception is that fraud is fraud. Discovering and controlling fraud is the responsibility of accountants, and if such discovery and control does not occur, then the SEC should step in and solve the problem. We tremble at the thought.

The *Management Accountant's Guide to Fraud Discovery and Control* and the workshops on fraud represent our initial contribution to the fraud auditing profession. We invite your comments and recommendations.

HOWARD R. DAVIA
PATRICK C. COGGINS
JOHN C. WIDEMAN
JOSEPH T. KASTANTIN

CONTENTS

CONTENTS

CONTENTS

MANAGEMENT ACCOUNTANT'S GUIDE TO FRAUD DISCOVERY AND CONTROL

1

INTRODUCTION

ABOUT THIS GUIDE

In designing the *Management Accountant's Guide to Fraud Discovery and Control*, the authors have included certain requisite investigative and legal materials necessary for the traditional auditor to be transformed into a new breed, the fraud auditor. The fraud auditor approaches the audit environment with a sense of controlled paranoia. He or she accepts few environmental facts without further testing and verification.

The fraud auditor relies on internal controls to provide a reference point and as well as a trail for certain transactions, but also knows that perpetrators of fraud are well versed in internal control systems. The fraud auditing technique is used to supplement internal control systems. Together, reliable internal control systems and fraud auditing provide the best overall protection for an entity's assets and resources.

The question is often raised as to the relative importance of detecting fraud versus preventing fraud from happening in the first place and prosecuting the perpetrator after it is discovered. It is the position of the authors that the primary purpose of fraud auditing is to control losses arising from perpetrated fraud. Patrick Coggins and John Wideman contend in their respective chapters of this book that all suspected cases of fraud should be investigated and documented with the intent of prosecuting the perpetrator. Howard Davia takes a similar position in the principal chapter of this book, "Fraud Auditing Standards, Methodology, and Classifications." The purpose of prosecuting the cases of suspected fraud is not to get even with the

1

perpetrator but rather to let other employees of the organization know that there are consequences to such action. The message is clear: If you commit fraud in this organization we probably will catch you eventually and you will go to jail for your crime. Mr. Davia makes it very clear that preventing fraud altogether is not economically feasible. The objective is to control fraud.

As with any control mechanism, management must weigh the relative costs associated with employing a mechanism of fraud control against the benefits derived. If an organization has a weak or nonexistent internal control system or if top management conveys to its employees a sense of "anything goes" by virtue of its own demonstrated attitudes, then fraud auditing will be a waste of time and money. If an organization has a good internal control system—that is, one that is capable of tracing transactions, fixing responsibility, and effectively communicating and monitoring management's policies—and top management fosters a reasonably ethical climate demonstrated by its own behaviors, top management might allocate 20% to 25% of its control system resources to fraud-auditing efforts. If an organization has an internal control system that is of uncertain effectiveness even within an ethical climate, top management should allocate at least 50% of its control resources to fraud auditing.

Peter Lucas of the *Boston Herald American* once wrote that "fraud is still a growth industry."

It has occurred to the authors that some readers may be contemplating fraud, in which case the *Management Accountant's Guide to Fraud Discovery and Control* may provide a few new ideas. Nevertheless, we believe that all persons who aspire to be effective in finding fraud and controlling it must also know how to commit fraud. Succinctly but tritely put, we believe that "it takes one to know one."

Throughout the *Management Accountant's Guide to Fraud Discovery and Control* we will show you situations that involve fraud and lead you to think about how fraud occurs. Through the presentation of discussion material and some case studies, we hope to teach you a few tricks. Most of our case studies (some of which are included in Chapter 8) are taken from actual cases of fraud. The cases have been sanitized and simplified for illustration purposes. Regardless of how unlikely some of the case studies may appear, you can be sure that they describe incidents that have indeed happened to someone, somewhere. Facts, names, and places have been changed. Any identification with real persons, situations, or events is purely accidental and is not intended.

We do admit to at least one flaw in this material, however, which is regrettably unavoidable. Since the most successful perpetrators have not yet been detected, we can't show you their best examples of fraud!

OBJECTIVES OF THIS GUIDE

The *Management Accountant's Guide to Fraud Discovery and Control* has five primary objectives:

1. To increase the sensitivity of readers to the existence of fraud, including the not-unlikely probability of fraud in their own everyday work environments. If you are to be successful in disclosing fraud, you must become sensitive to the very likely possibility that fraud will exist under every stone that is overturned. You must become observant and see every clue. You must become like that Indian scout who appears in the old Western movies. He usually has a wise, wrinkled face and wears an old top hat with a turkey feather in it. He notices every broken twig and every overturned rock. Considering these indicia (signs), he squints and slowly says, "Six horses, one limping, passed by here two hours ago."

It is not necessary that fraud hunters wear an old top hat with a turkey feather—a rooster feather is fine. However, if they are to be successful in discovering fraud, their attitude must be such that they recognize that fraud might be present in the very thing they are looking at, at any given time. They must assume the attitude suggested by the popular saying "If at first you don't succeed . . ." and resist the attitude expressed by former Office of Management Director David Stockman, who in a 1984 *Fortune* magazine interview said, "Some still think there are vast pockets of fraud, waste, and abuse out there [in the federal government]. In fact, nearly every stone has been turned over."

Experience has shown that in instances where fraud has been discovered, the people most surprised by the disclosures were those closest to the perpetrator, possibly friends, who were genuinely surprised by the events and circumstances, even though in retrospect many indicia of the perpetrator's fraud could be recalled.

Case studies will be presented which provide excellent illustrations of clear signs of fraud (known as indicia), which often go unnoticed except by the sensitive eyes of the fraud auditor. Although indicia of fraud do not necessarily mean that fraud is present, the failure to investigate such signs denies the firm the opportunity to discover fraud and may even leave potential perpetrators unable to resist the temptation to commit fraud in the future.

2. To provide training in the disclosure of fraud. Experience has shown that the disclosure of fraud is a responsibility generally not assumed by independent auditors. (This issue is discussed later in the text.) Accordingly, the average auditor is not trained or experienced in the fine art of fraud disclosure. Disclosures to date have frequently been inadvertent, discoveries made purely by accident. There is generally no official record of the events leading to the discovery so that there is little learning value available by retracing the steps leading to the discovery.

The day is rapidly approaching, if it is not already here, when auditors must assume that responsibility and must be subject-trained. We can envision a time when auditors will have to give post-audit opinions on the likely presence of fraud within the audit universe examined.

3. To provide training in investigative technique. The fundamental purpose of this objective is to train auditors to a minimum level of competence in what constitutes proper investigative procedures.

We contend that one of the current problems in fraud discovery is that auditors are functionally illiterate in the area of proper investigative procedures. Furthermore, investigators generally are not sufficiently well versed in auditing to deal with some of the complex issues that may surface in a fraud investigation. The result is that the auditor and investigator may fail to communicate their needs and the relevance of their findings to each other. Although our material is designed principally for auditors, it may also prove useful for investigators who wish to become competent in fraud auditing procedures. John Wideman, a criminal investigator, is the principal author of the text material relating to investigative procedures.

4. To provide training in the nature of evidence required to conclude the presence of fraud and to identify the individual or individuals responsible. The rules of evidence are highly technical in nature. We feel it is essential for the competent fraud auditor to be versed in the fundamentals of the rules of evidence. The materials addressing this topic were written by Patrick C. Coggins, a professor of law and ethics who also has experience in auditing and accounting procedures.

5. To provide training in the internal controls necessary to deter the occurrence of fraud, and their limitations. Notice, that we say *deter* the occurrence of fraud, not *prevent* it. To prevent fraud from occurring, although desirable, is impossible. Appropriate internal controls are essential in limiting the occurrence of fraud. Internal controls also enhance the detection of fraud. However, there are many frauds that are internal-control resistant. Some internal controls are not cost-effective. What we expect to do with internal controls is to raise the level of difficulty in practicing fraud, and to raise the risk of detection.

We do *not* plan to make you an expert on fraud. There is no such person except, perhaps, in the relative sense. We will, however, provide you with a balanced view on what is important on this subject. For those persons having a need for more intensive training in any of the topics covered, please contact the Institute of Management Accountants at 10 Paragon Drive; Montvale, NJ 07645-1760, or the Executive Education Series, Inc. at 4324 Drectrah Road R2; La Crosse, WI 54601.

Since the Treadway Commission issued its final report in 1987, several books, products, and seminars concerning fraud detection, deterrence, and control have appeared on the scene. In writing this book we have attempted to create a unique guide for those interested in increasing their fraud-auditing skills. It is intended to be a single-source reference for fraud auditors. To accomplish this the authors generally assume that the reader is already trained in basic accounting and auditing skills.

Recently we encountered an ad for fraud-detection software. For only $395 the ad claims to take the guesswork out of fraud detection. Fraud is a very personal crime. It often involves very talented individuals who perpetrate frauds in diverse and devious ways. Since software is rigid in its ability to handle data and since decision software to date has not been able to emulate the human thought process, we are skeptical about claims such as those made in this ad. That is not to say that such software would not or could not be useful to a fraud auditor. But the software itself is only a tool that contains a series of audit procedures much like those found in any internal control manual. The reason we bring this up now is that fraud is only just beginning to be recognized as the menace it really is. Those who wish to defend their companies against fraud are advised to become competent in fraud auditing, rather than rely on the skills and tools of others to protect them.

Although there are many people who will protest to the contrary, we believe it can be said that given the right circumstances, *anyone might commit fraud.* Luckily for most businesses, those right circumstances never arise. However, driven by need, greed, boredom, or whatever else motivates them, there are many who will find and seize opportunities to commit fraud. And quite often they are the nicest people. For instance, let us relate to you an interesting case involving the nicest man.

The story is a true one. It began sometime in 1973 or 1974. Charlie Brown (not his real name) was an extremely personable middle-aged man, well liked by everyone. After his retirement from the air force, he was employed by the government as an accounting clerk.

One day, Charlie announced to his many friends that a dear old rich aunt had died and that she had left him her sizable fortune. Soon after the announcement, it became obvious that Charlie was beginning to enjoy his new-found wealth. He would take many of his office friends out to lunch, always with cocktails, and always picking up the check. He joined the prestigious and expensive Illinois Athletic Club, where he also had a sleeping room. He bought luxury cars and an expensive condo in the Marina Towers, a landmark in downtown Chicago.

It was probably about two years after Charlie's aunt had died that two old friends were having coffee in a government cafeteria. One was an accounting supervisor, the other a building manager from Minneapolis who was in Chicago on business. The accountant was teasing his old friend because just a month earlier the building manager had been complaining that he did not have enough money in his financial plan for essential preventive maintenance. The accountant kidded his friend about the fact that, after complaining about his tight budget, he was spending large sums on nonessentials, such as cleaning venetian blinds.

The building manager looked at his friend strangely and asked, "What are you talking about?" The accountant repeated what he had said, and his friend told him he was completely wrong. He insisted that he had authorized no such spending. But further investigation disclosed that large expenditures had in fact been made for cleaning venetian blinds, and that they had been approved by the building manager. The building manager charged that the signatures authorizing the expenditures were forgeries.

It was then discovered that many similarly questionable payments had been made, involving various buildings and building managers. However, interestingly, although different vendor names were involved in the different building services provided, all mailing addresses on the questionable invoices bore the same post office box address. Investigation disclosed that the subject post office box was rented to Charlie Brown.

In his job as accounting clerk, Charlie had access to budgetary records for all federal buildings in a six-state area ranging from Ohio to Minnesota. Charlie would regularly scan the budgetary accounts for all federal buildings, noting particularly those that appeared to have excess funds. He would then prepare a phony purchase order, requesting building services such as venetian blind or rug cleaning, and forge the building manager's signature. The phony purchase order would then be put into the government's computer system as a duly authorized order for services due-in. Two or three weeks later Charlie would prepare a receiving report certifying that the service had been satisfactorily rendered, again forging the appropriate building manager's signature. In a week or so he would prepare and send in an invoice for the service performed. About a week or so later he would receive a government check in his post office box.

Easily identified through his post office box, Charlie pleaded guilty. He was subsequently indicted for stealing $300,000. Audit tallies showed that the amount of the theft was closer to $900,000. Charlie Brown's personal property was seized as partial repayment of the amount stolen; however, most of the money was never traced or recovered.

Charlie was prosecuted in a federal district court and found guilty. He was sentenced to a one-year prison term, with a work-release provision, much of which was satisfied by Charlie's pretrial confinement. This story seems to contradict the adage that "crime doesn't pay."

2

THE AUDITOR'S
RESPONSIBILITY FOR
FRAUD DETECTION
AFTER TREADWAY

At first blush, the topic of this chapter sounds like one that should simply recount the activities of the accounting profession, and the business and regulatory agencies since the Report of the National Commission on Fraudulent Financial Reporting (the Treadway Commission). The chapter title, however, contains some ambiguities that must first be resolved. In order to have a case of fraudulent financial reporting it is assumed that either someone within the reporting company or their independent auditors, or both in collusion, have issued a financial report containing false or misleading information concerning the company's financial condition or results of operations. Furthermore, from a legal viewpoint, in order to prove that fraud has taken place it is necessary that the perpetrator or perpetrators intended to defraud a third party, perhaps a creditor or potential investor.

As its title clearly states, fraudulent financial reporting is what the Treadway Commission Report was all about. And when fraud is discussed these days the conversation eventually leads to the role that the Treadway Commission has had in rooting out fraud. Yet there is considerably more to fraud than fraudulent financial reporting. The question is, shall we discuss fraudulent financial reporting? Or shall we discuss the auditor's responsibility for fraud detection? This is a much larger question.

To complicate the matter further, when we talk about auditors shall we refer to internal auditors or external auditors? Each group of auditors plays a different role in fraud detection, and each group serves a different master. The result is that these groups have varying interests in fraud and auditor responsibility for detecting it.

Fraud detection in general seems to refer to detecting fraud that has been committed within the company, but not necessarily by the company. The fraud we refer to here is fraudulent financial reporting. However, this topic can be slanted considerably one way or the other, depending on whether one's audience consists principally of internal auditors, external auditors, or some other financial professionals. The *Management Accountant's Guide to Fraud Discovery and Control* was written for the accounting profession; however, fraud means different things to different groups. If we were to restrict our coverage of fraud to internal auditing responsibilities, then the public accounting profession would probably not be interested in it, except in passing. If we were to concentrate on external auditors' responsibility to detect fraud, then the internal auditing profession might be interested but the topic would probably not be highly relevant to its members.

To make this chapter as orderly and yet as effective as possible, we will discuss two categories of fraud. We will explain the differences between the two categories, and then explain our views concerning the roles that internal and external auditors should play in dealing with both categories of fraud.

FRAUDULENT FINANCIAL REPORTING

The Treadway Commission addresses most of its efforts to the first category of fraud, fraudulent financial reporting. The Commission defines fraudulent financial reporting as *intentional or reckless conduct, whether act or omission, that results in materially misleading financial statements.* The Commission focuses on public companies.

The causes of fraudulent financial reporting include:

1. Incentives such as the desire to drive up the price of the company's stock, to satisfy investors' expectations, to postpone

dealing with existing financial difficulties, or for a variety of personal gain schemes such as compensation and promotion.

2. Pressures such as sudden declines in market share or sales, unrealistic budgets, or short-term economic performance objectives.

3. Opportunities that are too tempting to ignore, such as an inattentive board of directors, weaknesses in the internal control system or internal control staff, complex transactions, or accounting estimates.

The primary perpetrators of fraudulent financial reporting, not necessarily in order of frequency or importance; are sales personnel, accountants, decision-making middle managers, and top management. These persons either are drawn into their schemes by a soft ethical climate or, as individuals, foster a soft ethical climate that leads others into temptations that are too great, or too easy, to pass up.

Since the October 1987 Treadway Commission Final Report was issued several significant events have taken place both within the accounting profession and in the business world in general. Some of what has taken place has been very positive. Some has not. For example, during 1988 the Auditing Standards Board issued its *Statement on Auditing Standards,* numbers 53 through 61, all of which address the independent auditor's responsibility for conducting the audit and discovering fraud. (These are covered in detail later in this chapter.) Before the ink was completely dry on SAS 53–61, the GAO issued its report to the Chairman of the Committee on Banking, Finance and Urban Affairs, House of Representatives, titled *CPA Audit Quality.* The diatribe was printed in the March 1989 issue of the *Journal of Accountancy* without comment, with the exception of the following 78-word preface:

Following is the complete text of the General Accounting Office's report on its review of the quality of CPA audits of 11 savings and loan associations that failed in the Dallas area. The report is reprinted here to respond to the GAO's recommendation that the American Institute of CPAs communicate its contents to all AICPA members. The Institute urges all members to read this report carefully and consider whether its criticisms and recommendations are applicable to their practices.

The tone of this preface speaks for itself. In addition to other blistering criticism of the accounting profession, the report demanded that the AICPA rewrite its 10-year-old *Audit and Accounting Guide for Savings and Loans Associations* to respond to the vast changes in the savings and loan industry during that 10-year-period.

Just to make sure no one got the idea that the savings and loan industry contained the only examples of fraudulent financial reporting, the previously nearly unblemished credit union industry discovered its largest fraud-related disaster when, on November 4, 1988, the Franklin Federal Credit Union of Omaha, Nebraska, failed. Subsequent examination revealed that the president of Franklin had misappropriated in excess of $39 million in deposits over his 13-year career as leader of the organization. His motto was "A hand up, not a hand out." One congressman, on reflection, asked, "Or was it a hold up?"

What makes the failure of a federal or state chartered financial institution even more difficult to deal with is that many of these organizations are subject to three different levels of audit:

1. The internal auditor, armed with the industry's internal audit manual.
2. The independent external auditor armed with audit programs and appropriate AICPA industry audit guides.
3. The regulatory agency auditor armed with the agency's audit guide and programs.

Is it any wonder congress and the general public scratch their heads and wonder, often out loud or in print, if the auditing profession ought to be federally regulated?

RESPONSES TO TREADWAY RECOMMENDATIONS

In a March 1989 article in *Management Accounting* magazine (Sweeney, Robert, "Executive Summary: The Report of the National Commission on Fraudulent Financial Reporting," March 1989), author Robert Sweeney prepared an executive summary of the

Treadway Commission Report. Recommendations were directed at four audiences:

1. Public companies.
2. Independent Certified Public Accountants.
3. The Securities and Exchange Commission and other regulatory and law-making bodies.
4. Education.

Public Companies

The recommendations directed to the top management of public companies called for top-management education on the causes of fraudulent financial reporting and the development of codes of corporate conduct.

According to the March 1989 article in *Management Accounting*, a survey of some 8500 companies revealed that 42% had already adopted written corporate codes of conduct. The article did not say how many of these were adopted as a result of the Treadway Commission. As heartening as this fact is, an almost equal number of respondents did not have a written corporate code of conduct and had no plans to adopt one in the near future.

One might note that, as with many of the recommendations made by Treadway, some are objectively measurable and others are not. Of course, one could ask what difference it makes whether the recommendations are objective. We believe it does make a difference for the following reasons:

1. The Treadway Commission was not intended to be a smoke-screen defense against federal regulation of the accounting profession. It was, however, a necessary precedent in demonstrating to congress that the accounting profession intends to spearhead an effort to clean up financial reporting problems.

2. As such, the recommendations had to be clearly written and had to address the heart of the issue of fraudulent financial reporting. We believe the recommendations satisfy those conditions.

3. In addition to having substance, the recommendations must *appear* to have substance, even to the eyes of a casual lay observer. It is, after all, the casual lay observer who votes for the members of congress who oversee appointments of certain regulatory officials. It is also the casual lay observer who watches the evening news and reads the newspapers and news magazines for juicy tidbits about the latest fraud scandal.

4. If the recommendations are to be proven useful in retrospect, the measure of their usefulness will likely be in terms of whether they precipitated a reduction in the occurrence of fraudulent financial reporting. And for this to work there must be a measurable cause-and-effect relationship between the implementation of the recommendations and the hoped-for outcome. The objectivity of the recommendations, in effect, will determine the worth of the Treadway Commission's efforts.

The recommendations concerning internal controls were fairly predictable and, to a certain extent, were not objective. The recommendations addressed such issues as effectiveness of the internal control staff and their internal control activities, the objectivity of the internal audit function, consideration of nonfinancial audit findings on the company's financial statements, and coordination of internal audit activities with the independent public accounting audit function. Although these recommendations are laudable, they are not new.

Incidentally, the same *Management Accounting* article mentioned earlier reported that 46% of the companies responding to the survey indicated that they did not have a separate internal auditing staff. Presumably this means that the internal audit function in smaller companies is being taken care of by the accounting department or the controller.

There are several recommendations directed to independent audit committees that are relevant, innovative, and objective. Herein lies the heart of the Treadway Commission Report:

1. The board of directors of all public companies should be required by SEC rule to establish audit committees composed solely of independent directors.

2. Audit committees should be informed, vigilant, and effective overseers of the financial reporting process and the company's internal controls.

3. All public companies should develop a written charter setting forth the duties and responsibilities of the audit committee. The board of directors should approve the charter, review it periodically, and modify it as necessary.

4. Audit committees should have adequate resources and authority to discharge their responsibilities.

5. The audit committee should review management's evaluation of factors related to the independence of the company's public accountant. Both the audit committee and management should assist the public accountant in preserving his or her independence.

6. Before the beginning of each year, the audit committee should review management's plans for engaging the company's independent public accountant to perform management advisory services during the coming year, considering both the types of services that may be rendered and the projected fees.

The *Management Accounting* survey revealed that 79% of the responding companies had independent audit committees, although only about half of the smaller companies even had audit committees.

Recommendation numbers 1, 3, 4, and 6 are objective. Numbers 1, 3, and 4 taken together will perhaps create the best line of defense against fraud in general and against fraudulent financial reporting specifically. Board members are nominated for their positions for reasons other than their managerial competence or technical knowledge more often than not. A strong knowledgeable, independent audit committee becomes the third party to the audit process. The other two parties are the company's management and the independent auditor. Again, numbers 2 and 5 are well intentioned and sound good but are probably not objectively measurable; hence their effectiveness after the fact will be difficult to correlate to the results of the adoption of the recommendations.

THE AUDITOR'S RESPONSIBILITY FOR FRAUD DETECTION

According to a February 1989 article in the *Journal of Accountancy* (Bull, Ivan, and Sharp, Florence Cowan, "Advising Clients on Treadway Audit Committee Recommendations," Feb. 1989), a significant number of CEOs and audit committee heads shared two concerns:

1. They believe that both the time demand and the legal liability exposure of audit committee members will likely be increased as a result of the Treadway Report. One chairman referred to the liability exposure as enormous and said he is resigning from all directorships of public companies. If this concern proves to be well founded, competent people who are willing to serve on audit committees may become harder to find.

2. They are concerned that recommendations for informed, vigilant, and effective oversight of the reporting process and internal controls, and of the quarterly reporting process, may encourage what one CEO terms "micro-management" by the board of directors.

In a June 1988 *Financial Executive* magazine article (author not named, "The Treadway Commission—What Happens Next?", June 1988), six auditing experts were interviewed concerning the Treadway Commission Report. One panel member said, "One of the criticisms of the Treadway Commission Report is that it wanders rather widely from fraudulent financial reporting. It addresses much larger issues. My own personal concern is that you get very quickly into morality and religious belief when you start talking about ethical behavior. . . . If the audit committee thinks its role is to get down into the bowels of management, to interview lower-level employees about the code of business conduct or anything else, then I think the audit committee is moving into a management function— and I submit that that is a mission impossible."

The *Journal of Accountancy* article mentioned earlier (Bull, Ivan, and Sharp, Florence Cowan, "Advising Clients on Treadway Audit Committee Recommendations," Feb. 1989), cited several qualities needed for audit committee service:

1. Financial statement literacy including an understanding of how business activities are reflected in the financial statements.

2. An ability to recognize potential problems through analyses and discussions.
3. An understanding of the auditing process—internal and external.
4. The disposition to ask probing questions and get answers to them.
5. Skill in communicating with managers, statement preparers, and auditors.
6. Natural curiosity.

Although the SEC Practice Section specifically prohibits CPA firms from recruiting board members for audit clients, CPAs can help identify reports useful to the audit committee, such as:

1. Quantified plans and budgets.
2. Monthly financial reports, with explanations for budget variations.
3. Details of unusual transactions and adjustments.
4. Internal audit reports.
5. CPA audit reports and letters.

Two additional recommendations concerning the annual financial report to stockholders actually are ways of implementing the previous recommendations:

1. All public companies should be required by SEC rule to include in their annual reports to stockholders, management reports signed by the chief executive officer and the chief accounting officer and/or the chief financial officer. The management report should acknowledge management's responsibilities and how these responsibilities were fulfilled, and provide management's assessment of the effectiveness of the company' s internal controls.

2. All public companies should be required by SEC rule to include in their annual reports to stockholders a letter signed by the chairman of the audit committee, describing the committee's responsibilities and activities during the year. Other recommendations in this area seem to be either intuitively obvious or a rehash of already existing practices.

Independent Certified Public Accountants

In the area of responsibility of the independent public accountant there were several critical recommendations. After all, the general public, no matter how vehemently the public accounting profession protests to the contrary, looks to the independent auditor to find fraud and protect the investing public from charlatans. The recommendations admonished the Auditing Standards Board to revise standards of responsibility to detect fraudulent financial reporting, including the provision of guidance to CPAs for assessing risk and pursuing detection when risks are identified. Without question, the actions of the ASB subsequent to the issuance of the Treadway Report are among the most visible. As mentioned earlier, the ASB has issued 13 new *Statements on Auditing Standards*, addressing most of the Treadway's recommendations. The statements are as follows:

53. The Auditor's Responsibility to Detect and Report Errors and Irregularities.
54. Illegal Acts by Clients.
55. Consideration of the Internal Control Structure in Financial Statement Audit.
56. Analytical Procedures.
57. Auditing Estimates.
58. Reports on Audited Financial Statements.
59. The Auditor's Consideration of an Entity's Ability to Continue As a Going Concern.
60. Communication of Internal Control Structure Related Matters Noted in an Audit.
61. Communication with Audit Committees.
62. Special Reports.
63. Compliance Auditing Applicable to Governmental Entities and Other Recipients of Governmental Financial Assistance.
64. Omnibus.
65. The Auditor's Consideration of the Internal Audit Function in an Audit of Financial Statements.

All things considered, these pronouncements are a substantial improvement over those that they replaced. In some cases the pronouncement topics have been promoted to the status of separate publications. Given the litigation-oriented society in which we operate, the attitudes of investors concerning risk shifting and the malpractice liability insurance industry, the new statements should be quite effective. And they are most assuredly a visible response to Treadway's recommendations.

Two recommendations directed to the auditor's report are worthy of discussion and of perhaps a little criticism.

1. The ASB should revise the auditor's standard report to state that the audit provides reasonable but not absolute assurance that the audited financial statements are free from material misstatements as a result of fraud or error.

2. The ASB should revise the auditor's standard report to describe the extent of internal accounting control. The ASB should also provide explicit guidance to address the situation where, as a result of his or her knowledge of the company's internal accounting controls, the independent public accountant disagrees with management's assessment stated in the proposed management report.

With regard to the first recommendation, the ASB has issued a new standard auditor's report. The report is considerably different from its predecessor; however, it is still silent in regard to fraud, irregularities, and illegal acts. Granted, these are addressed in the new SASs, but the fact remains that Treadway's intent was explicitly to communicate the auditor's level of responsibility for detecting fraud. This still has not been done, and perhaps with good reason.

The second recommendation all but puts the independent auditor in an adversarial role vis à vis the client. This is a new and different way for CPAs to deal with clients who do not agree with their assessment of internal controls. Of course, the disagreement may result in the auditor's being fired and replaced with a new firm. Presumably, the purpose of the replacement is to secure a report that is not critical of management's internal control system. This seems to be a problem-ridden recommendation. SAS 60 responds to this recommendation.

Interestingly, in the *Financial Executive* panel discussion article mentioned earlier, one panel member said he felt that external auditors should decrease compliance testing on internal controls. "The external auditor needs to stop thrashing around the bowels of our client's accounting systems and move to the areas where he or she has real expertise. For it's also in those areas where the unreliable financial reporting occurs. Even crooks need good data."

Securities and Exchange Commission and Other Regulatory Agencies

Many of Treadway's recommendations deal with enforcement issues. Among others are the following:

1. The SEC should seek explicit statutory authority to bar or suspend corporate officers and directors involved in fraudulent financial reporting from future service in that capacity in a public company.

Although the intention of this recommendation is clear, it is not certain that it is workable within our permissive society.

2. Criminal prosecution of fraudulent financial reporting cases should become a higher priority.
3. The SEC must be given adequate resources to perform existing and additional functions that help to prevent, detect, and deter fraudulent financial reporting.

It seems that the message conveyed by these recommendations is twofold. First, if we are going to get excited about controlling fraudulent financial reporting we have to have enforceable and meaningful sanctions that can be imposed against perpetrators. Second, the SEC must be able to do its job efficiently and effectively. SEC registrants and their independent CPAs must have confidence that the reporting and disclosures that are required of them are necessary and that they will be acted upon in a swift and unbiased manner. Furthermore, registrants must feel confident that their reports are being processed in an objective manner, without their suffering any unwarranted harassment or intimidation.

Having to do directly with CPA firms that serve SEC clients, the Commission recommended that CPA firms which audit public companies be required to undergo a peer review and an independent oversight function approved by the SEC, such as the SEC Practice Section of the AICPA's Division for CPA Firms. The recommendations also include enforcement action when a public accounting firm fails to remedy deficiencies cited in the public accounting profession's quality assurance program.

Without regard to action on the part of the SEC, the AICPA now requires any firm that performs so much as one audit to subject itself to peer review. According to Joe Sperstad, former Executive Director of the Wisconsin Institute of Certified Public Accountants, this requirement seeks to find and eliminate "One Audit Charlie" (That is, practicing CPAs who only conduct one audit per year and thus are assumed to lack competence in auditing). The cost of the review is about $1000. The additional requirement that the CPA firm become a member of the SECPS is already in force by the AICPA.

Several of Treadway's recommendations seem to be more political pleas or statements than serious recommendations.

1. Parties charged with responding to various tort reform initiatives should consider the implications that the perceived liability crisis holds for long-term audit quality and the independent public accountant's detection of fraudulent financial reporting.
2. The SEC should reconsider its long-standing position; insofar as it applies to independent directors, that the corporate indemnification of officers and directors for liabilities that arise under the Securities Act of 1933 is against public policy and therefore unenforceable.

Education

Overall, the Treadway recommendations had to be and appear to be two-dimensional. They had to address immediate problems with immediate solutions. The outcry from the general public and their echoes, the congress and news media, demand swift and sure remedies to fraudulent financial reporting. Of course, no matter how diligent the accounting profession becomes, it will be difficult if not impossible to cure all the fraudulent reporting problems that exist and will surface during the coming years.

One of the misconceptions held by the general public concerning disclosures of fraud is that the disclosures themselves are a sign of flaws in the system. Quite the contrary is actually true, depending on how the fraud is discovered and disclosed. If the discovery is made and documented in the course of an audit and its disclosure is made through the proper channels, this is a sign that the system is working the way it is supposed to. In other words, fraud is out there waiting to be discovered. If those who are responsible for finding it are indeed finding and disclosing it, then congress and the general public should be pleased, not outraged.

The second dimension to the Treadway Report is that which looks into the future. During the past 30 years or so the education system has concentrated on producing technically competent business persons, including accountants. In earlier times students were educated in arts, letters, and sciences. Those who demonstrated managerial competency were promoted into management. Therefore, managers had to be both skilled in the industry in which they were employed and able to demonstrate competence in managing resources.

Now we train managers in college. These bright-eyed wonders exit academia armed with management skills taught by professors who generally have little or no management experience outside the classroom. These graduates have high expectations of wealth, fame, and mobility. They also have two very negative characteristics. First, for the most part they have not achieved a level of maturity consistent with either their expectations or the responsibilities with which they will be charged by their employers, who have equally high expectations of their expensive recruits.

Second, many of these graduates have little or no interest in what they have been trained to do. What they are interested in is megabucks. Many of our graduates today look at two factors in choosing a major. First is the latest starting-salary survey. If they can find a profession that is even remotely interesting to them, they will probably pursue it if it is high enough on the salary list. Second is the amount of resistance anticipated on the path to that profession. The more difficult the program, the less likely candidates are to pursue it.

With regard to education the accounting profession has a few advantages over other business-related professions. If an accounting graduate wants to optimize his or her career opportunities, then a professional designation is a must. The best known is the Certified Public Accountant (CPA), followed by Certified Management Accountant (CMA) and Certified Internal Auditor (CIA). There are a whole host of designations that have recently surfaced in addition to these.

Now that the word is out that specialization is necessary because of the complexity of the business environment, we can expect to see certificates in many business professions in the future. For now at least, the accounting profession can serve as a quality control mechanism for accounting education. If an accounting graduate gets through an accounting program and cannot pass the appropriate examination, or for some reason elects not to take one, then the graduate is doomed to an inferior status and salary within the accounting profession. Of course, this is not to say that the person will not become a resounding success in some field other than accounting.

Furthermore, even if the graduate passes the CPA examination, he or she still has to satisfy the state accountancy board's experience requirement. And, after certification and licensing, the CPA has to maintain continuing education requirements or risk losing the license to practice.

The Treadway Commission rose to meet the education challenge. The Commission also addressed the problem of ethics in education. The jury is still out on whether we can successfully teach good ethics in college which will produce graduates who practice good ethics in the workplace. In fact, it will be many years before we have a legitimate verdict on this matter. In the meantime, there are several recommendations that focus on this long-term aspect of fraudulent financial reporting.

The Commission has asked educators and those licensing accountants to put out the word that fraudulent financial reporting is a no-no. The business education community has been charged with increasing students' analytical, problem-solving, and judgment skills and to emphasize ethical values, all in an effort to curb fraudulent financial reporting. The Commission has even gone so far as to ask business schools to overhaul their faculty rewards system to encourage faculty to develop their own personal competence in skills that would help to prevent, detect, and deter fraudulent financial reporting.

Realizing the short-term nature of legislated solutions to the fraudulent financial reporting problem, Treadway had enough foresight to address one of the long-term solutions, which has already been mentioned: education, certification, and licensing. In its simplest form this solution conveys the message to the entering accountant that what is right and what is wrong is a matter of fact rather than opinion which depends upon personal value systems to provide appropriate guidance. Then we propose testing the accountant before we certify him or her. The test presumably will become evidence that the participant, at least at the time of examination, was aware of what constituted acceptable behavior. With licensing, we can ensure that only those who have been tested, who comply with continuing education requirements, and who do not violate the certifier's code of ethics will behave in an acceptable manner.

Another March 1989 *Management Accounting* article coauthored by Alfred King, then Managing Director of the Institute of Management Accountants, suggested that anyone who issues financial reports be certified by a professional society that maintains a code of ethics. The article proposed that the CMA certification might be appropriate for such persons. The authors' intent in the article was not to usurp authority from either the CPA or the CIA designations, but rather to call attention to their opinion that in most instances of fraudulent financial reporting, one or more chief accounting or financial officers were not doing their jobs. Certification would at least ensure that the responsible party was completely informed as to the level of responsibility being assumed in the issuance of the company's financial statements.

TRANSACTION FRAUD

We believe the Treadway Commission has provided a framework for effectively dealing with the fraudulent financial reporting problem. It is clear that the public accounting profession has accepted responsibility for detecting material occurrences of such fraudulent reporting. The Treadway Commission, however, has failed to address the other category of fraud, which we refer to as transaction fraud. The public accounting profession steadfastly declines responsibility for detecting transaction fraud. This creates a series perception problem that it is generally understood that Treadway deals with all fraud and the public accounting profession accepts responsibility for detecting all fraud, not just fraudulent financial reporting.

For auditors there is no easy solution to the public's misunderstanding. It is difficult for auditors to explain to the lay public that to expect a CPA to discover fraud in a customary audit effort is like expecting a person to go both north and south at the same time. The required audit techniques and methodology are so unlike that to do both would be tantamount to performing two audits. Perhaps more to the point, the public client of ordinary audit services, who is paying for only one effort, cannot expect to get a transaction fraud discovery effort in the bargain.

Of course, even if it were possible to explain to the public why ordinary audits have little likelihood of discovering fraud, we doubt that their indignation would be placated by that understanding. An explanation would not assuage their concerns that transaction fraud might be eating into their profits. Only an independent, fraud-specific audit would do that. Unfortunately for clients desiring one, fraud-specific audits are usually not available from CPAs.

For example, it is well to consider that the audit procedures used by independent auditors and fraud auditors have dramatically different audit objectives. The objective of the ordinary auditor is to express an opinion on financial statement balances. All of his or her audit procedures are designed to test the reliability of those balances and the records which produce them. This auditor's approach is more or less macro in scope. That is, he or she is ordinarily not over-interested in the many individual transactions that contribute to financial statement account balances, unless, of course, their erroneous recording would serve to materially distort the balances.

To the contrary, the fraud auditor follows an almost reverse methodology. The objective is not to verify financial statement balances. Accordingly, his or her audit procedures are not designed to do so. With a specially heightened sensitivity for indicia of fraud, this auditor culls through transaction detail that the ordinary auditor does not have time for. Once significant details are found, the fraud auditor, who is also cross-trained in investigative skills, doggedly pursues and builds upon minute indicia discovered until he or she has a clear case of prosecutable fraud.

The fraud auditor's training also includes the accumulation of mental templates for the myriad variations of transaction fraud. These templates are invaluable in recognizing the often scant evidence of fraud that is normally encountered. Of course, when it comes to fraud that does not involve a client's accounting entries, the ordinary audit stands little or no chance of discovering it.

Fraud Auditing Standards

One Solution the Treadway Commission did not mention was the introduction of fraud auditing standards. Clearly, there is an ongoing problem with independent CPAs who offer attest services. They must go up against perpetrators of fraud who have several advantages. The perpetrator is usually an expert in the system, particularly the internal control system within which he or she operates. In fact, the perpetrator has the additional advantage of looking from the inside of the system out. The perpetrator knows where the system is strong and where it is weak.

Perhaps the first problem the fraud auditor faces in accepting responsibility for discovering fraud is the lack of the proposed "General Standards for Fraud Auditing" and "Standards of Field Work for Fraud Auditing." Until they are developed, it will be difficult for the practice of fraud auditing to develop systematically and effectively. Chapter 7 introduces our initial proposal.

Obviously, there must be generally accepted measures and guidelines which fraud auditors and others can reference for the purpose of evaluating the adequacy of fraud auditing service, if any degree of responsibility for discovery fraud is to be assumed.

The perpetrator may also have the advantage of being a full-time employee of the organization. He or she is there day in and day out, observing not only the system of internal controls but also those people who operate the system. The perpetrator is often able to override the system because of his or her apparent trustworthiness, longevity, and charming personality.

The perpetrator operates with the knowledge that traditional auditors, both internal and external, employ sample testing during their examinations. A prudent and conscientious perpetrator is aware of the scant odds of being detected, given the sampling system. He or she knows that the auditor cannot perform a 100% examination of transactions. To do so would be prohibitive in terms of man-power and money and would probably be a wasted effort, given that relatively few transactions are fraudulent.

Fraud auditing standards would serve two purposes. First, their very establishment would serve as formal notification that there are two types of audit services. Attest services address the financial statements taken as a whole. They concentrate on offering assurance that the statements are accurate and properly stated within certain tolerance limits and subject to materiality constraints. Fraud auditing standards would be virtually unconcerned about the financial statements taken as a whole. They would instead provide for standards of conduct of specific fraud auditing procedures. In a sense, the fraud auditor would have a relatively free reign in the organization. The primary purpose of the fraud auditor would be to find fraud, rather than to express an opinion that it is probable that fraud doesn't exist within the system.

3

STANDARDS OF ETHICAL CONDUCT

DEFINITION

Any discussion of fraud would be incomplete without discussing what constitutes acceptable behavior on the part of an organization's employees. Among other things, they are generally expected to be ethical and moral. However, the terms *ethical* and *moral* have different meanings to different people. What is ethical and moral to one person may be unethical and immoral to another. Accordingly, it is absolutely essential that top management of every organization carefully consider, and publicize for all employees to know, the *standards of conduct* for their organization. This recommendation was also made by the Treadway Commission on Fraudulent Financial Reporting.

What are standards of conduct? This is our quick definition:

Standards of conduct are those criteria which an organization adopts as constituting acceptable and unacceptable behavior on the part of its employees, and which may be used as the basis for disciplinary action.

Key to this definition are the terms *criteria* and *basis for disciplinary action.*

What a Standards of Conduct Statement does for an organization, no matter how small, is to advise employees—all employees, management included—what employees may do, and what they may not do as employees, in their relationships with others, particularly those others with whom their employer does business.

28

EXAMPLES

Let's consider a few examples of what can happen. Assume that you are a purchasing officer for the company you work for, and that your employer has *no* Standards of Conduct Statement. A salesman for a major supplier visits your office one morning.

1. You talk for a while, and when you feel like smoking you find that you are out of cigarettes. He offers you *a* cigarette. Do you take it? Why? Why not?

2. You accept the cigarette offered and thank the salesman. It is a new package of cigarettes that he hands you. It is your favorite brand. He says, "Keep the pack! I've got a whole carton in my sample case." Do you? Why? Why not?

3. You keep the pack, thanking him. You feel its $1.50 cost is insignificant. You go to light your cigarette and find that you have no matches. He takes out an attractive cigarette lighter and hands it to you. You light your cigarette and attempt to hand it back. He says, "Keep it! I have more." Do you? Why? Why not?

4. You estimate the lighter's value at about $25 and figure that it's part of the supplier's normal promotional expense. You decide to keep it, and thank him. You talk for an hour and notice that it is twelve o'clock noon. He does too. He suggests that you and he go to lunch and continue your conversation. You agree. You have a fine lunch and two martinis. He insists on picking up the check for about $40. Do you allow him to pay? Why? Why not?

5. After lunch, back at your office, the salesman is showing you his company's catalog. You like a product that his company sells, and which your company needs to buy. The price appears competitive. You tell him that you wish to place an order for $10,000. He suggests that you may wish to increase the order to $15,000. He states that for a $15,000 order customers get an all-expense-paid trip for two to Acapulco. You increase the order to $15,000. It's an extra three months' supply, but your company can use it. Your wife always wanted to go to Acapulco, and now you can go together—for free!

6. Acapulco is great. After your return, with your suntan still with you, your salesman friend visits you again. This time he asks you if you would like to go to Europe, all expenses paid. All you need to do is order $50,000 worth of Product X, of which your company uses a great amount. The price is a bit higher than the competition's, but you decide to buy anyway. You tell him you would like to visit Italy.

Sound familiar? It happens every day in just about every industry. And regardless of how you may have responded to the questions of propriety in each of the six instances described above, there are *no* standards of propriety to guide your organization. It is not our intention here to suggest standards to you. What we do strongly recommend is that your organization *carefully consider the likelihood for employee gratuities, and draw a line between what is acceptable and what is not.* These standards of conduct for employees should be required periodic reading for all employees.

The consequence of not issuing a standards of conduct is that someday a business will find itself in a situation where an employee in a key position has caused the organization significant financial harm, and no disciplinary action will be possible.

The following quotation was taken from a speech given about 15 years ago. It is no less relevant today than it was when it was delivered by John C. Biegler, senior partner of Price Waterhouse & Co., before the Harvard Club and the Harvard Business School Club of Philadelphia on January 12, 1977:

> Uncertainty is the enemy of ethics. Many corporate employees have behaved improperly in the misguided belief that the front office wanted them to. If standards are not formulated systematically at the top, they will be formulated haphazardly and impulsively in the field. . . . While the independent auditor's external review is an indispensable supplement to a corporate system of internal controls, it is not a substitute for it. Management must take the major responsibility for implementing and improving them.

There is an adage that says something like, "You don't get nothing for nothing." It is worth remembering. For every gratuity you take, there is a quid pro quo (Latin: *something for something*, or *this for that*). Some organizations have adopted very rigid standards of conduct that allow employees to accept no gratuities. Others tend to allow gratuities that fall below a set monetary amount, such as $10 or $20, for example. Some allow an employee who is offered a free lunch to accept it without being embarrassed, provided it falls within certain parameters.

Perhaps the most important thing that is accomplished by limiting the gratuities an employee can accept is that it tends to sensitize that employee to the quid pro quo theory. Consider, for example, the following scenario, which actually happened. Only the details have been changed, for obvious reasons.

Assume that you live in New York City and that you are employed by a large national general construction contractor. You are a senior project manager for your company, with the authority to make major contractual adjustments. You find it necessary to visit Mr. Jones, a major subcontractor in the Los Angeles area.

At the close of the day he says, "Let's go out and have dinner." You agree to go if you can pay. He accepts. At dinner an extremely attractive young woman, Marsha, who seems to know Mr. Jones, comes over to your table. It appears that they are good friends, and she has dinner with you and Jones. Forgoing dessert, Jones remembers a late business appointment and rushes off, but suggests that you and Marsha have dessert and an after-dinner drink on him.

Marsha is very charming. You and she dance, and end up going to her home where you become intimate with her. Later that evening you return to your hotel. The next day you cannot get her off your mind, and that evening you decide to return to her home. She answers the door and is surprised to see you there. You suggest that she invite you in, and she replies, "Who is paying for tonight?" What do you do? (If you wish, you may change *she* to *he* and *Marsha* to *Mark*.) As mentioned, this story is not fiction. Only the names have been changed. In the real case, the incident hit the newspapers in the man's home city *before* he arrived. He was married. Enough said.

Obviously, the big question in the acceptance of gratuities of any kind is in the quid pro quo that is expected from the gift recipient in return. Logically, if the gratuity has worth the giver must recover its cost in the products he sells. Accordingly, might we then consider the gratuity in the same category as a kickback? Why not?

Consider this situation: You are a new internal auditor for the Bluebird Corporation, only recently graduated from college. One day you find yourself reviewing invoices for the purchase of various housekeeping supplies used by the corporation. It is a low-priority audit, but has been scheduled as a part of your familiarization training. You pick up an invoice from the XYZ Corporation for a large order of detergents, priced at $10,325, to be used for general plant cleaning and maintenance purposes. Bored, you notice the usual things one would expect to find on an invoice of this sort: 12 50-gallon drums of detergent XXX, 20 5-gallon containers of industrial floor wax, and so forth. You are about to put the invoice back into the file when a notation in the "Remarks" section of the invoice catches your eye. It says, . . . "Deliver television set to Harry Kari residence at 624 Market Street." You determine that Harry Kari is the Bluebird purchasing agent who made the purchase.

Checking further, you find that the XYZ Corporation is a new vendor to Bluebird, and you also notice that the unit prices paid to other vendors for identical items purchased in the recent past were about 10% lower. You check with your audit supervisor and tell him what you have found.

After pondering the situation, put yourself in the position of the audit supervisor and respond to the auditor who has just presented you with this observation.

We recall quite vividly the experiences of a good friend who worked as a general traffic agent for a major railroad. Every month Marty would visit the traffic department of a major manufacturer that shipped a significant amount of freight over the rail lines of the company Marty worked for. Every month Marty was expected to take the entire traffic department out to a long, expensive lunch, complete with cocktails. To facilitate the monthly party it was necessary to take these employees out in two shifts, so that all could attend. Marty claimed that if he were to miss a month, freight tonnage shipped on his railroad would decline substantially. In effect, the railroad that employed Marty was kicking back a substantial sum each month to obtain the business of the major manufacturer.

The federal General Services Administration, rocked by widespread fraud in the late 1970s, found itself in a situation in which many key contracting personnel had been accepting significant gratuities—many could easily be called kickbacks. But they soon found that without clearly defined standards of conduct with regard to the acceptance of gratuities, no administrative action could be taken against the individuals involved, even when the gratuities were quite large. In one instance, a GSA contracting representative, influential in approving significant contract changes for a major government contractor was found to have received many gratuities. The GSA employee had been entertained in grand fashion every time the contractor's representative visited Washington, or when he visited the contractor's plant. The GSA subsequently reacted by declaring that *no* gratuities would be tolerated and that there would be *no* exceptions. This posed more than one problem when employees were the recipients of small token gifts, such as desk calendars, all of which had to be returned.

Greed has been part of the human race as long as the human race has existed. The objects of greed that could formerly be confined to what we could see in our immediate neighbors and neighborhood have now been expanded to include the whole world and will no doubt go further as technology permits us to see beyond. Marketing has increased the velocity of new product introductions. With each new product comes an added opportunity for greed. What he or she has, I too must have.

ETHICS WITHIN THE ORGANIZATION

Ethics, in the context discussed here, refers to the behavior and conduct that is practiced within an entity or organization. As such— even though we generally think of ethics as being good—within this context, ethics are neither good nor bad. Ethics refers only to present behavior or conduct within an entity or organization. If an entity's ethics are questionable or bad, per se, then it means, succinctly put, that the behavior or conduct of the constituents of the entity is not in the best interest of the community as a whole and may not even be in the best interest of the entity itself. We believe that the entity is incapable of behavior or conduct. Only individuals are capable of behavior or conduct.

The entity has but one line of defense in a society in which the behavior or conduct of individuals is in question because of personal value systems resulting in questionable ethics: it must establish standards of conduct for its constituents. Standards of conduct are a clear statement of the entity as to what behavior or conduct is permissible and what is not. Presumably, if the standards of conduct are violated by a constituent, the constituent must be punished.

STANDARDS FOR EMPLOYEES

The behavior of employees within an entity is influenced by a variety of factors. One source of such influences is the diverse cultures and backgrounds both within and without most employees' family units. It may not always be correct or safe to assume that employees will act in a manner consistent with the best interest of the entity. Consider two factors: first, most employees, because of their positions within the company, probably have very little understanding of the entity or its purpose and activities taken as a whole. This sort of information tends to be restricted to top management. Second, even if employees in general know or think they know the whole story about the entity, they will, because of their diverse cultures and backgrounds, have diverse interpretations as to what is in the best interest of the entity. Standards of conduct, clearly written and clearly and frequently articulated to all employees, provide a defense for the entity in that each employee knows what behavior and conduct will be tolerated and what will not be tolerated.

4

INTERNAL CONTROL

DEFINITION

It can be said that *anything* that protects an entity's assets or entitlements from loss or misstatement may be considered to be an internal control. Businesses and other entities have always used internal controls in an attempt to protect themselves against losses resulting from fraud.

The exposure draft dated March 12, 1991, and issued by the Committee of Sponsoring Organizations of the Treadway Commission, entitled *Internal Control—Integrated Framework*, defines internal control as

> the process by which an entity's board of directors, management and/or other personnel obtain reasonable assurance as to achievement of specified objectives; it consists of nine interrelated components, with integrity, ethical values and competence, and the control environment, serving as the foundation for the other components, which are: establishing objectives, risk assessment, information systems, control procedures, communication, managing change and monitoring.

The exposure draft further recommends that the policy of management reporting on internal control to external parties be expanded, perhaps to the extent of making such internal control reporting mandatory for all publicly held companies. An illustrative report is included which suggests appropriate language to be used in the transmittal letter for the report. The language is not radically different from that which may be found in the independent auditor's report, except that it relates exclusively to internal control matters and is signed, in the illustration, by the CEO and CFO of the company.

Appendix C to the exposure draft contains informational tools, a reference manual, and an illustrative evaluation for a hypothetical company. All of this material is very useful in helping an entity to conduct an evaluation of its internal control system. Overall, the *Integrated Framework* is an outstanding document and tool. It will be most interesting to track its final release and survey its implementation by businesses.

One might ask the question, "Why are internal controls necessary in the first place?" There are several possible responses; for example, "We wish to establish a system by which transactions and other activities affecting the business can be tracked in order to better manage the business." Another might be, "To establish a set of guidelines for our employees, to instill a habit of doing things consistently the way management feels they should be done." Perhaps a more cynical response might be, "To protect our company's assets from loss and abuse." And, of course, "To prevent fraud." All of these responses have some degree of appropriateness.

The *Integrated Framework* cites five deficiencies that have frequently been found in organizations that have experienced a control failure:

1. Lack of integrity, or ignoring ethical values, on the part of top management.
2. A weak or negative control environment.
3. Failure to link top-level objectives with objectives for operating and support units.
4. Poor communication within the organization.
5. Inability to understand and react to changing conditions.

Internal controls may be as simple as the requirement for two signatures on a check, which subjects a payment to the scrutiny of at least two persons. Or they may be complicated and intricate, as in a large automated system. Internal controls may be special discrete requirements, such as the requirement for a bank reconciliation to be prepared by someone other than the custodian of the checkbook.

Or they may be an integrated part of an operating system, such as a provision that incoming mail be opened on a table in full view of others, and that the contents of remittance envelopes be split and the cash sent to the cashier and the documentation to accounts receivable.

From a fraud auditing perspective, the primary objectives of internal controls are to

1. Make it difficult for fraud to occur;
2. In some cases, to make it impossible for fraud to occur; and
3. Where fraud does occur, to make it possible to discover the fraud and to identify those responsible for it.

Those formulating internal controls usually begin with an end objective in mind—that is, to assure that some action is done properly or to stop some wrong from occurring. The desired end objectives are achieved by *requirements* to process transactions in a prescribed way.

IMPORTANCE TO FRAUD AUDITORS

It is absolutely essential in the conduct of any audit, including a fraud audit, for the auditor to know and evaluate existing internal controls. Although there is currently no statement of field audit standards for fraud auditors, one will undoubtedly be written which will be quite similar to the second *Standard of Field Work* published by the AICPA for independent auditors. It provides that

A sufficient understanding of the internal control structure is to be obtained to plan the audit and to determine the nature, timing, and extent of tests to be performed (AICPA AU Section 150.02).

The fraud auditor reviews an internal control system to determine its strengths, weaknesses, and redundancies for the purpose of

1. *Locating audit testing.* Obviously, the weaker areas, or areas of greatest risk, will be tested more aggressively than the stronger or low-risk areas.

2. *Improving the internal control system.* The fraud auditor is responsible for making constructive recommendations for tightening control and suggesting control alternatives.

3. *Determining redundancies, inefficiencies, and controls that are no longer effective, or are not cost-effective, and which should be changed or deleted.* There is a tendency to retain the vestiges of old control systems that no longer serve a purpose, are costly to operate, and tend to dilute the effect of needed controls.

SHOULD INTERNAL CONTROLS BE DESIGNED TO PREVENT FRAUD?

An internal control system ordinarily *should not* be designed to, nor be expected to, prevent fraud from occurring. The infinite possibilities for fraud, including the growing incidence of collusion between parties to commit fraud, make the design of preventive controls impractical and often extremely extravagant.

Unfortunately, there is no simple formula that can be used for determining what constitutes an adequate system of internal control. Every internal control system should be unique and should be designed to serve the circumstances and environment of the entity within which it functions. Every entity requires a different internal control system, because no two entities are alike. Normally, factors such as the size of an organization, the degree of automation of its activities, the vulnerability of its assets, its geographical dispersion, and its employee turnover rate, are among those that dictate the sophistication needed in an internal control system.

Internal controls should ordinarily be designed to

1. Make it difficult to commit fraud;
2. Make it easier to detect fraud when it does occur;
3. Be cost-effective;
4. Fix accountability; and
5. Be a deterrent to fraud by making its discovery likely.

Historically, internal control system design objectives included making its host system fraud resistant. However, although many contemporary systems still strive to achieve this objective, it is *not* recommended.

There will be instances when it may be *necessary* to design controls aimed at preventing fraud even though they may not be "cost-effective". Such instances include those in which an entity would be in such peril of fraud that there is either no alternative, or the lack of controls might actually invite it. An entity in which employees routinely handle large amounts of cash might be such an example. However, such instances should ordinarily be the exception rather than the rule, and should be carefully considered.

The prevention of fraud has been—and is—the objective of many contemporary internal control systems. The theory expressed by advocates of the comprehensive systems is that "it is better to lock the barn door before the horse leaves, than to leave it open and spend your time searching for the horse."

If the subject were as simple as keeping horses from voluntarily wandering out of their barns, we would have to agree. In cases of fraud, however, assets do not wander away. They are taken. And the locked barn door does not deter determined horse thieves.

However, the locked-barn theory for internal control has been popular. In fact, up until 1977 the American Institute of Certified Public Accountants advised:

> Reliance for the prevention and detection of fraud should be placed *principally* upon an adequate accounting system with appropriate internal control. . . . It is generally recognized that good internal control and fidelity bonds provide protection more economically and effectively [than auditing] (*italics added*) (AICPA Codification of Auditing Standards and Procedures 1, 110.06).

Section 110.06 was superseded in January 1977 and the quoted portion eliminated in revisions to it; however, it illustrates the thinking that prevailed in the design of internal control systems of that era and, to a significant degree, is *still persuasive* in their design. Obviously, fidelity bonds would protect an insured only for those frauds that were discovered and to the extent that monetary losses were proven.

To these entities that still depend "principally upon an adequate accounting system with appropriate internal control" and who *do not* supplement the internal control with proactive fraud auditing, we can only wish them luck. They will need it. Of course, if they are hosting a benevolent thief, they may never know what fraud is costing them.

DESIGN STANDARDS

Internal controls are essential to the containment of fraudulent activities. They are the primary defense against fraud and should, in one form or another, be employed by every business entity. It is unthinkable *not* to have internal controls. However, they should be subject to at least the following design standards.

Internal control systems should:

1. Be cost-effective.

2. Be efficient.

3. Provide reasonable protection against the occurrence of fraud.

4. Provide an audit trail that allows detection of any fraud that may occur.

5. Fix accountability for fraudulent transactions.

6. Use directed auditing as an effective, economical alternative.

There will be occasions when the fraud auditor is aware that fraud is occurring, may be occurring, or could occur because of system weaknesses, but concludes that it is *not* cost-effective to implement the internal controls necessary to stop it. That is, the cost of the estimated actual fraud, or estimated fraud potential, is simply not worth the cost of internal controls needed to stop it.

An interesting illustration of this sort of dilemma occurred in the mid-1970s during a review and evaluation of the Internal Revenue Service's revenue accounting system which controlled the processing of billions of dollars in tax receipts.

Auditors reviewing the system's controls discovered that a possible fraud was being conducted by a significantly large number of taxpayers. The suspected fraud involved the simple transposition of numbers representing taxes withheld on the tax return filed. The transposition served to raise the amount of wages withheld. For example, if a taxpayer's actual amount withheld was $2,095, he or she would indicate on the tax return that the amount withheld was $2,905, which would result in a refund check $810 in excess of the taxpayer's entitlement.

The error worked for the suspected fraud perpetrators because the IRS, in the mid-1970s, had not fully automated its collection system to capture amounts reported as withheld, and were not comparing amounts reported on W2 forms attached to tax returns with amounts reported on the tax returns.

Although the solution to this problem at first appears obvious, the IRS, to its credit, did not rush to judgment. Before undertaking changes to its tax system's internal controls, it first did several things. Through a statistical sampling of tax returns, the probable loss resulting from the transpositions was determined. As we recall, the loss in tax revenues was estimated at about $14 million a year. However, the minimum cost of comparing amounts reported by employers as withheld, with amounts reported as withheld on tax returns, was about $20 million a year. Consider that there were many millions of tax returns that would have had to have been checked manually at that time.

Because of the negative cost benefit of implementing internal controls to stop the loss of revenues, the IRS properly decided not to implement the necessary additional controls. However, the IRS continued to monitor the transposition losses every year through statistical samples to assure itself that systems controls continued to have a negative cost benefit.

Although the IRS system is an extremely large dollar system, the principles expressed in this example are the same for a system of any size. That is, before electing to implement internal controls to stop a loss, or possible loss, first determine the cost benefits of the controls. Incidentally, there was one other factor that influenced the IRS not to make any changes. Many taxpayers were apparently making transpositions which cost them—to the government's advantage— about $20 million a year. These taxpayers were never advised of their errors.

Generally speaking, auditing is not normally thought of as an internal control. It can, however, be a very powerful and effective control. When designing internal control systems, or reevaluating them, proactive fraud auditing should be considered together with fixed in-place procedures. The most cost-effective of the two should be the designer's choice. Consider, for example a situation in which—although the review of an accounting system disclosed a weakness in internal control which, if exploited, would allow fraud to occur, probably without detection—no instances of fraud have been found. In such a situation, the fraud auditor or system's analyst is faced with a dilemma. That is, should he or she:

1. Alter the operating system to provide the protection desired, even though the changes will be disruptive, and somewhat costly?

2. Make *no* changes to the operating system, and accept the risk of fraud, but institute required proactive fraud auditing to monitor the risk and the cost of the fraud?

Both are viable options, and neither should be automatic. The decision must involve an estimate of the *total* cost of option 1, the likelihood of fraud, its likely unrecoverable cost under each option, and the cost of the proactive fraud audit.

Where proactive fraud auditing is elected to serve as an adjunct to internal control, there must be a commitment from the internal auditors that the required audit procedures *will* be performed as stipulated, without deviation.

A PROGRAM FOR CONTROLLING FRAUD

Fraud can be combatted through an appropriate mix of three initiatives:

1. Increased awareness, or sensitivity to fraud.

2. Appropriate audit programs creatively designed to disclose evidence of criminal activity and visibly conducted to constitute a deterrent to fraud.

3. Appropriate internal controls designed to limit the opportunity for fraud, to constitute a fraud deterrent, and to improve the ability to detect fraud.

Why not attempt to eliminate fraud with internal controls? It would be impossible to eliminate the occurrence of fraud even with the best preventive measures. Consider the following reasons:

1. The ingenuity and daring of perpetrators cannot be anticipated. Too many frauds occur off the books for one thing, which would not be deterred by internal controls. In addition, many frauds occurring on the books, such as those involving employee collusion, would occur despite the best of internal controls.

2. It would be prohibitively expensive to try to even limit significantly the occurrence of fraud with internal controls alone, much less eliminate it.

3. An overaggressive effort would disrupt normal business and productive processes.

The Three Es

In setting out to control fraud, the so-called controller must conceive a marriage of internal controls, auditing, and financial management accounting, which is: *E*fficient, *E*conomical, and *E*ffective.

Such a marriage is admittedly more easily described than accomplished and, frankly, is *rarely achieved*, even by organizations particularly concerned with the problem of fraud.

Organizations that seek to rely on internal controls as the major bulwark against the occurrence of fraud can easily find themselves with controls that are expensive, burdensome, and have a deleterious effect on their operations.

As indicated earlier, the American Institute of Certified Public Accountants is changing its views on the subject of how to deal with fraud. Until recently, in its Statement on Auditing Standards, it held that independent auditors could not (and hence would not) assume responsibility for the detection of fraud. Auditing is an appropriate internal control in lieu of hard controls designed into operating systems. The advantages of auditing are several:

1. Auditing seldom affects the productivity of an operating system.
2. Auditing is reliable when competently and scientifically conducted.
3. Auditing cannot be defeated by employees acting in collusion.
4. Auditing is flexible.

Systems designers responsible for fraud-proofing operating systems should routinely review their operating systems to determine that the internal controls (1) remain effective, (2) remain cost-effective, and (3) continue to provide comprehensive coverage. In so doing, they should constantly be asking the question, "Can I improve this control by designing a hard control into the operating system, or by periodically auditing to determine if a weak area is being penetrated?" They may be surprised to find that existing internal controls that have been designed into their operating systems to strengthen perceived weaknesses, are resulting in an overkill of the problem.

If a system weakness is discovered in an operating system, the tendency is to install hard controls that operate continuously to eliminate any risk of loss. However, all controls have a cost. Rather than a rush to that solution, alternatives should be considered first. For example, if the discovered weakness has the potential for fraud or other loss, but the loss up to this time is minor or nonexistent, then it is wise to *consider* watching it with audit observation, rather than to needlessly encumber the operating system just to rule out the possibility of loss.

DESIGNING AN INTERNAL CONTROL SYSTEM

Flow Charting

The existing operating system should be evaluated by persons who have in-depth knowledge of that system. Obviously, the evaluator should have as much or greater knowledge than an employee, somewhere in the organization who has extensive knowledge of his or her segment of operations, and who may be inclined to commit fraud.

As a technique, we recommend flowcharting as many operations of the entity involved as reasonably possible. The flowchart presents a visual picture of the flow of documents and eases comprehension of a process or segment of operations. In the use of flowcharts, it is true that a picture is worth a thousand words. A flowchart makes it much easier to see weak points in an operating system and to determine the controls that are necessary to strengthen them.

Assets

All entity assets should be carefully reviewed, and their susceptibility to conversion should be carefully evaluated. Cost-effective controls should be designed to protect them. One caution here is necessary: It is important not to be obsessed with controlling assets such as cash *to the exclusion of other convertible assets.* Many of the frauds that are being detected do not involve cash at all.

Systems designers should not limit themselves to the protection of assets on the books. Consideration must also be given to unrecorded entity assets which could be diverted. Unrecorded assets, at times, could include proceeds from vending machines, cafeteria proceeds, scrap inventories, accounts receivable which have been written off, and so forth.

Liabilities

Liabilities should be reviewed and evaluated for ways that dishonest employees could manipulate them for their own gain. It is often difficult to conceive of ways that liabilities per se could be converted to a perpetrator's benefit. One example is the overstatement of accounts payable. When the overstated amounts are paid, the perpetrator contacts the payee, calling his or her attention to the error and requesting a refund, which is then intercepted and converted.

Operating Accounts

All operating accounts should be reviewed for clues as to possible opportunities for fraud. In one case, for example, cafeteria receipts were being diverted by a perpetrator. A review of operating accounts would have disclosed the company's participation in a subsidized cafeteria program. An alert internal control system analyst would have inquired further into the particulars of the subsidy and provided controls to protect the income generated. Past income earned from any source, including scrap sales, vending machines, cafeterias, and so forth, is a clue to convertible valuables which must be protected.

Financial Management

A *responsive financial management system* is essentially a useful combination of *accounting* and *information* systems. Such a system is the foundation of a good internal control system. Many frauds have gone undetected simply because the entities affected did not know they were hemorrhaging dollars. Good financial management simply means, as a minimum,

1. Comprehensive control over all assets and liabilities;
2. Unit costing of operations to the maximum extent possible; and
3. Definitive financial plans that fix spending responsibility with managers responsible for spending.

There are many entities that have notoriously poor accounting systems as far as preventing fraud is concerned. Perhaps the best evidence of this is the often-heard report of an entity that finds itself in financial difficulties resulting from fraud that has been going on for years. We are convinced that a good financial management system will disclose many clues of a significant management fraud which may be festering.

Business for-profit entities, relatively speaking, often have less of a problem than do not-for-profit entities, in which unit costing is rarely practiced. However, even in many for-profit entities unit costing is not adequately practiced. There may also be instances in which an influential perpetrator may impair an internal control to allow his or her fraud to go undetected by the existing systems.

Hotline

Every entity should establish a mechanism that allows employees, or others with knowledge of fraud or other wrongdoing, to communicate those ideas, anonymously if they choose, to a designated authority. In fact, the very existence of a publicized hotline communicates to all interested parties that they should be alert to fraud and that the subject entity is serious about stopping it. A hotline provides an opportunity for anonymous reporting which otherwise might not exist.

SUMMARY

A system of internal controls has been the long-standing defense against fraud. We encourage the continued use of well-thought-out internal controls that are efficient, effective, and economical. Furthermore, those internal controls periodically should be tested to ensure that they remain efficient, effective, and economical. Fidelity bonding, long held to be a defense against fraud, addresses only fraud that is discovered. The most effective line of defense against fraud includes fraud-specific auditing procedures. These procedures may be conducted by internal staff or by external auditors under a fraud auditing engagement.

5

THE NATURE OF FRAUD

The objectives of this chapter are to discuss and examine the nature of fraud and to get to know more about the perpetrator. Success in discovering fraud will increase proportionately with knowledge of these topics.

This chapter was written primarily for the layman who is not knowledgeable of the legal system or the justice system. Although definitions and comments provided herein are suitably correct and appropriate for the layman, readers requiring more precise legal definitions should refer to Chapter 11 "Perspectives and Procedures for Documenting Evidence of Fraud."

WHAT IS FRAUD?

There are many definitions for fraud, depending on who provides the definition. However, they all tend to embellish the following basic definition taken from *Webster's New Collegiate Dictionary*, which defines fraud as

> an intentional perversion of the truth in order to induce another to part with something of value or to surrender a legal right.

For the fraud auditor or investigator, since he or she must concentrate on finding the guilty party or parties, we could change the definition in the following manner:

> *Fraud* always involves one or more persons who, with intent, act secretly to deprive another of something of value, for their own enrichment.

All parts of this definition of fraud are worth remembering, in that fraud involves essentially five elements:

1. There is a *perpetrator.*
2. The perpetrator has acted with *intent.*
3. Someone has *parted* with *something of value.*
4. The person who has parted with something of value *doesn't realize* at the time that he or she has done so.
5. The perpetrator has *benefited* from the act.

Intent to Commit Fraud

Many auditors seem not to fully comprehend the requirement that to *prove* in a court of law that fraud has occurred, it is necessary to show that the person, whom available evidence indicates committed the fraud, intended to commit the fraudulent act. This is particularly important if prosecution is expected. The authors believe that significant fraud should *always* be prosecuted.

It is our recollection in forwarding cases for prosecution that even in seemingly well-documented cases of fraud there seemed never to be enough evidence to please prosecutors. Moreover, as anyone who has been involved in compiling evidence to prove fraud knows, such proof is often very difficult to come by. Even when convictions were obtained, prosecutors often have been heard to say that they had trouble proving intent. In cases when conviction *was* obtained, any shortcoming in proving intent is often evident in the severity of the convicted party's sentence.

In prosecuting a perpetrator charged with a single case of fraud, who does *not* have a criminal record, it can be anticipated that the defense will make an issue of the defendant's lack of intent, and may win an acquittal if the evidentiary package is not sufficient.

A U.S. attorney once told us that he was always reluctant to prosecute a single case of fraud against a defendant with no criminal record. "However," he would advise, "give me more than one instance of fraud—three is better than two, and I'll get a conviction every time." Obviously, evidence of multiple crimes more clearly shows the perpetrator's intent.

What sort of person commits fraud? We would like to be able to tell you that the average perpetrator is probably a male, of a shifty appearance, in need of a shave and a haircut, wearing a black shirt with a white tie, exhibiting a periodic muscular spasm which causes him to jerk his head as though his collar were too tight, and sneering a lot. But we cannot. If anything, we might suggest that you look elsewhere when you spot such a person. Fraud perpetrators tend to be the least suspect. This characteristic provides excellent cover for the cautious perpetrator.

Do only men commit fraud? No. Federal Bureau of Investigation figures show that between 1976 and 1985 the number of women arrested for embezzlement increased 55%, compared with a 1% decrease for men. Fraud arrests among women shot up 84% in the same period, nearly twice the rise among men. A May 29, 1987, *Wall Street Journal* article, "Broken Barrier: More Women Join Ranks of White-Collar Criminals," reported:

> As white-collar crime among women has increased, some telling contrasts between male and female offenders have become apparent. A recent Yale University study found, for example, that white-collar men who steal typically take far more money than women—an average of 10 times more.
>
> The study also found that female white-collar criminals, who are largely clerical workers, tend to get involved in simpler fraud, and usually act alone and out of concern for their families. Many of their male counterparts, by contrast, tend to be conspiring managers. And while men tend to use stolen funds for luxury items rich as sports cars, women embezzlers may be motivated more from a need to make ends meet. However, . . .
>
> A former female insurance broker in St. Petersburg, Florida, who owned several companies and a 24% stake in a Florida bank, began a three-year prison sentence in 1985 after embezzling more than $1.8 million from escrow accounts she managed for a Philadelphia insurance company.

Do offenders look any different from non-offenders? No. In fact, many offenders are the nicest people. The government worker in Chicago, for example, who stole $900,000, was extremely well liked by his co-workers. After "his rich aunt died" and left him a sizable inheritance he was known to take them out frequently for expensive lunches. He was friendly and very nice looking. He was not known to wear black shirts or white ties, and he shaved every day.

WHAT IS FRAUD?

If not personal appearance, what then do you look for? Ordinarily, there are few if any clues in a person's countenance that would indicate he or she is a white-collar criminal.

If we were to recommend looking for anything, it would be a person's life-style. Many white-collar criminals cannot resist spending their ill-gotten gains. The government worker in Chicago, for example, suddenly became quite extravagant, attributing his good fortune to his inheritance. His sudden generosity to his fellow employees, investments in cars, condominiums, and athletic club memberships, should have made people suspicious. However, it did not. People tend, perhaps subconsciously, to prefer to accept explanations such as inheritances, or Las Vegas winnings. The proactive fraud auditor or investigator, however, cannot afford to accept explanations of sudden good fortune to explain unusual spending patterns. An offender who embezzled $10 million recently was caught only when an investigator visited his home and knew he could not afford to live there on his salary. There are a number of instances in which male offenders were suspected when they began wearing $500 suits that they could not afford on their salaries.

Are white-collar criminals content to steal just once? No, not usually. This is the *most useful knowledge that the fraud auditor or investigator can possess.* If a fraud auditor or investigator can depend on any one characteristic of the white-collar criminal it is that he or she is, or will be, a repeat offender.

Accordingly, when any indicia of fraud are discovered, (1) the person (or persons) identified with those indicia should be determined, and (2) any audit or investigation should be extended to examine all aspects of that person's (or persons') activities for an extended period of time. If more evidence of fraud is discovered, it will confirm the auditor's original findings and more than likely provide evidence of multiple offenses so needed to prove intent. If no additional evidence is discovered, the original findings of fraud indicia should be reexamined.

By the same token, evidence of additional crimes perpetrated by the same person can improve the case for the prosecution. Prosecuting attorneys are frequently concerned with the difficulty of prosecution when evidence is scant or when there is evidence of only one crime. Successful prosecution of a fraud case requires that the prosecutor clearly show the defendant's intent to commit fraud. Scant evidence often fails to do that. In addition, one instance of reasonably documented fraud is often not sufficient to convince a benevolent jury to convict a defendant with a reasonably clean record. Rather than a lack of desire, a lack of sufficient evidence is perhaps most frequently the reason that so many business victims of fraud choose not to prosecute, and that many judges tend to be lenient. Of course, prosecution of perpetrators is one of the best psychic internal controls a business can employ and is always recommended where fraud is material.

We have a simple theory about persons who would perpetrate fraud, that drives the effective fraud auditor's detailed audit program. It is "Only thieves commit fraud; and a thief is a thief is a thief." Simply said, it means that when evidence of a fraud is discovered, it is very likely that there are more frauds and more evidence where that came from. The fraud auditor should immediately assume that the suspect, if he or she is in fact a thief, is very likely to be guilty of many frauds. Subsequent audit review should then be concentrated in the suspect's area of responsibility. Anytime there is hard evidence of a fraud, or indicia of fraud, the fraud auditor probably has his or her suspect. All previous activities the suspect has been involved in, for a reasonable period of time, should be examined. If a suspect is in fact innocently involved, the auditor's failure to disclose additional evidence may clear him or her. If, however, additional evidence of fraud is disclosed, the perpetrator can be appropriately dealt with. Where any indicia of fraud is found, always examine very closely the the activities of the person suspected.

Personal Nature of

Regardless of who the perpetrator may be, or how many perpetrators there are, the fraud auditor is reminded that fraud is a very personal thing, and always involves one or more persons acting with a criminal intent to covertly take possession of the property of another. Accordingly, in auditing for fraud, unlike traditional auditing, it is essential to keep in mind always that a person is the object of the hunt. A favorite tactic of the fraud auditor is to determine *who* has an opportunity to commit fraud, and then review to determine that the opportunity has not been abused. And, when any indicia of fraud is discovered, the fraud auditor must determine *who* may have been involved in producing that indicia, and then must intensify the review of events involving that person.

The personal aspect of fraud auditing is most distasteful to many traditional auditors. Insufficient attention to the personal aspect of a discovered fraud is often the prime reason that white-collar thieves are not prosecuted, or not successfully prosecuted. That is, the auditor or investigator simply has not made a sufficiently strong case against the perpetrator to enable successful prosecution. Without clear evidence of "who did what" there is often no case.

There is a short poem by Rudyard Kipling which should serve all fraud auditors well in collecting evidence of a suspected fraud. It is worth memorizing.

> I keep six honest serving men
> (They taught me all I knew);
> Their names are What and Why and When
> And How and Where and Who.
> *Just So Stories*, 1902

Obviously, any proactive audit or investigative work which involves specific individuals, *should be conducted with the utmost discretion.* The auditors or investigators involved should be careful to cover their work by at least seemingly undertaking other work to mask their more limited objective and to preclude embarrassment to the *innocent* persons who are suspect, and to themselves.

THE AUDITOR VERSUS THE CRIMINAL INVESTIGATOR

On the subject of fraud it is worthwhile to examine the normal relationship between auditors and criminal investigators.

To begin with, the auditor is generally considered to be proactive, whereas the criminal investigator is considered to be reactive. That is, the auditor normally performs in an audit universe where there is no evidence that a crime has occurred. The criminal investigator normally reacts to evidence that a crime is suspected, or has occurred, and performs to search for and compile evidence of the crime. The auditor rarely performs independently in a crime scene unless assistance is requested by a prosecutor or criminal investigator. The criminal investigator infrequently, except in specialized programs, performs in a setting where no crime is known or suspected.

The auditor and the investigator each have unique skills common to their professions. The auditor is primarily skilled in management and accounting, and the investigator is primarily skilled in the recognition and collection of evidence needed to prosecute a crime. (The many skills possessed by persons in each of the two professions have been necessarily condensed here.)

Unfortunately, there are relatively few persons who have significant cross-training in these professions. The result, frankly, tends to be an unsatisfactory approach to dealing with fraud. It also tends to explain why auditors frequently fail to recognize evidence of crime when it is encountered in conducting traditional audits. In addition, their lack of exposure to crime tends to make auditors insensitive to indicia of crime.

A minor but interesting example relevant to this point once occurred after internal auditors had reviewed an automobile rental activity. They observed in their audit report that many of the automobiles were experiencing rather low tire mileage, and speculated on the probability that it was due to rough usage. They recommended an increase in rental rates for the rough users in order to recover the tire costs resulting from premature wear-out. None of the auditors suspected the truth of the matter, that tires were being stolen. In this instance the low tire mileage was an indicia of a possible crime that was there to be "seen," but was not "seen.".

THE FRAUD AUDITOR

The fraud auditor is a sort of hybrid who is fundamentally a traditional auditor by education and experience, but who has been cross-trained in rules of evidence and investigative skills and sensitized to more readily recognize fraud indicia. Using these combined skills, fraud auditors are uniquely equipped to function in a proactive mode, to search out and find fraud. It is always advisable that persons trained and experienced in fraud auditing be substantially employed in fraud auditing, in order that they may continually sharpen their fraud-finding skills and enhance their sensitivity to the indicia of fraud.

6

FRAUD-SPECIFIC AUDITING

Throughout this text we have frequently used the term *auditing* in a broad sense to define the practice of *searching for fraud*. We find it a simple term to describe the search process, and its usage should not be confused with established and disciplined traditional auditing practice, or the persons professionally involved therein. Accordingly, our accountant and other non-auditor readers should rest assured that our words apply equally to them if they have a responsibility to search for fraud.

Incidentally, although it may be contested by many management accountants, it is they—not auditors—who are generally considered by management to be primarily responsible for deterring or detecting fraud. Professional auditors are secondarily responsible. It is the accountants who have the responsibility to design and monitor internal control deterrents to fraud. And, it is they who have an ongoing opportunity to detect fraudulent accounting transactions as they are processed, and after they may have occurred.

Whenever I discuss the subject of fraud-specific auditing I have a recollection of a visit I once made to the holy shrines located at Nikko, Japan. As a young soldier I found it interesting that they placed two massive Korean stone dogs at each side of a shrine's entrance. The dog to the left was always carved with a fierce snarling face. It was intended that evil spirits would be deterred from entering, much as internal controls are designed to prevent fraud from occurring. But, being realists, the Japanese allowed that some evil spirits might slip past the snarling dog on the left. So, the dog on the right was carved with a peaceful sleeping countenance, to allow the evil spirits that did manage to enter to leave.

Fraud-sensitive accountants are aware that it is impossible to preclude fraud from occurring with internal controls, no matter how comprehensive they are. And, in lieu of a "dog on the right," fraud-specific auditing is used to root out the fraud that has eluded the entity's internal controls. Fraud-specific auditing is quite unlike traditional auditing, and, unless independent accountants are engaged to specifically search for fraud, it is unreasonable to expect them to discover fraud in the same time frame allowed for their normal financial statement verification audits. This should become apparent as you read Chapters 6 through 8. Similarly, unless internal auditors adjust their traditional audit practices they will not be particularly successful at finding fraud. Fraud-specific procedures and a questioning mind set are fundamental to finding fraud.

INTRODUCTION TO FRAUD AUDITING

This chapter, unlike other chapters, is not based on an "existing body of knowledge," primarily because one does not exist.

The material is a condensation of lecture material created for classroom use. "Fraud-specific" auditing is relatively new, but there are clear signs that it is an emerging practice. Accordingly, writing a text on the subject is difficult since we do not yet have the benefit of tried, true, and long established procedure so essential to the preparation of texts.

In a classroom environment, the material presented herein would normally be accompanied by a lecture sufficiently expanded to assure understanding by all attending. In classes composed of accountants, auditors, and criminal investigators, the material presented is always "improved" by the experiences and ideas that are contributed by the participants.

Many of the definitions, practices, tactics, and opinions expressed herein are those of the author, and are largely derived from extensive and varied personal audit and investigative experience with *actual* fraud. Not all of the many cases that served as our learning experiences were prosecuted, or prosecuted successfully. Hence, "under the law" no formal "finding" of fraud was ever made for many of the cases. It is important here to recognize, however, that the courts do not pass on the merits of "cases" of fraud; rather, they pass on the guilt or innocence of those who may be accused of fraud. The significance here this is that even though there frequently is ample evidence to know with reasonable certainty that fraud has occurred, there is often insufficient evidence to convict anyone of the crime, at least beyond a reasonable doubt.

The author's knowledge of fraud, as described in this chapter, was gained largely from on-the-job experience. Most of it was acquired in the position of audit director of a large government agency, known as the government's "business agent," which was experiencing pervasive fraud. The agency's business activities could be described as a microcosm of businesses and institutions located throughout the world, both for-profit and not-for-profit. Hence, they constitute an invaluable learning experience for auditors and others who are interested in recognizing and controlling fraud. The agency involved (the General Services Administration), with billions of dollars at its disposal, leased office space; constructed, modified, renovated, bought, sold, rented, and managed buildings; purchased immense amounts of personal property; maintained warehouses; operated supply distribution systems; maintained extensive computer operations; purchased and operated vehicle rental fleets comparable to the largest of private car rental companies; maintained massive finance and accounting operations; had numerous large petty cash funds (e.g., over $25,000); administered extensive personal travel and transportation, maintained a 27,000-employee payroll, contracted for and managed large communications systems, directed manufacturing operations, and so forth.

Initially, like those of most businesses, the audit staff was simply not sensitive to the fraud risk. Although there was a staff of about 200 professional internal auditors otherwise effectively employed in traditional audit roles, as well as a sizable staff of criminal investigators, there was no perception of a significant fraud problem. Later, with the advantage of hindsight, it was obvious that an audit failure had occurred. The pervasive fraud that was subsequently discovered in seemingly unending varieties, had been there to find all the time. The auditors, considered well trained and experienced by most criteria today, were in fact not experienced or trained in fraud-specific auditing, nor were they being programmed to perform fraud-specific audits.

Things changed rapidly subsequent to the first few accidental disclosures of significant fraud. Fraud-specific audit activity was initiated, tentatively and ineffectively at first. But with continuing discoveries of fraud, audit activity became more aggressive and effective. In fact, post mortems of audit failures became perhaps the most enlightening of learning experiences. There was no such thing as a "worthless audit." Even the failures provided lessons to be learned. The trick was not to make the same mistake twice. With the expertise gained from experience, the ratio of fraud discoveries to audit efforts increased dramatically, and successful prosecutions followed as improved evidentiary packages were delivered to prosecutors.

Examining, recognizing, and assembling (ERA) sufficient relevant evidence to convict a perpetrator of fraud could be described as what fraud auditing is all about. This handbook, in its relative brevity, attempts in essence to suggest to the person who wishes to discover and successfully combat fraud (1) what to examine, (2) how to recognize fraud indicia, (3) what constitutes evidence of fraud, and (4) how to proceed with the accumulation of relevant and substantial evidence.

The limitations of this handbook, so desirable for general comprehension of the subject, also limits a more expansive discussion of concepts, tactics, issues, and most important, the greater use of case studies for illustration purposes. Auditors, as well as others seriously interested in learning more about discovering or recognizing fraud, should either enroll in one of the Fraud Workshops offered by the Institute of Management Accountants (IMA) as part of their Professional Education Program (PEP), contact the authors for class schedules, or, if enough persons are interested, arrange in-house training.

All auditors, controllers, and many accountants have a responsibility to determine whether there is fraud in their work environments. They should be asking themselves, "Can I afford to allow fraud to be 'accidentally' discovered?" "Can I afford to learn fraud-specific auditing the hard way, through experience alone?" "How many opportunities will I have to fail and still survive?" Learning about fraud penetration in your environment "accidentally," and learning fraud-specific auditing from experience can be a very costly and unforgiving process.

Any discussion of ways and means of auditing to discover fraud should logically first consider the following questions and answers:

Question: Will the discussion material be derived from an existing, well-established, audit methodology?
Answer: No.

Question: Why not?
Answer: It will not be so derived because there is *no* existing, established methodology for fraud auditing. Furthermore, there are *no* generally accepted fraud audit field standards, or generally available criteria that normally guide traditional auditors in the pursuit of their craft.

Question: Why is this so?
Answer: There is a lack of such methodology and standards because effective fraud auditing is generally not being practiced. Incredible and disturbing as this observation may appear, it is nevertheless reasonably certain, even though there are auditors who might argue otherwise. Please note that the key word is *effective.*

FRAUD—PERNICIOUS AND LARGELY IGNORED

We cannot overemphasize the fact that entities throughout the world do not adequately recognize the seriousness of their exposure to fraud. The result is that he or she who would commit fraud has, more or less, carte blanche to do so. All entities are at risk, but few perceive the serious gravity of that risk. The case in point is illustrated by a humorous story involving three children who were discussing what they planned to be when they grew up. One said he should be a doctor. Another said she planned to be a lawyer. The third child said that he would like to become a white-collar criminal. That evening he told his mother and father about his career plans and they soundly admonished him. Shaking long fingers at him they explained that "crime does not pay." Of course, he ignored them, and today is doing very well working as a government contractor.

All attempts at humor aside, there are compelling reasons for those who are not bound by moral restraints to choose a career of white-collar crime. There are reasons so compelling, in fact, that more and more persons are practicing it. What is most alarming is that this pursuit is attracting sophisticated practitioners. Consider the remarks made by the U.S. Department of Labor Inspector General in his March 31, 1990, semiannual report, wherein he comments on fraud involving pension and welfare plans:

> Fraud and racketeering in pension and welfare plans are not the exclusive province of labor union officials or ethnic stereotypes. Today, we face *a new generation of racketeers disguised as attorneys, accountants, bankers, benefit plan administrators, investment advisors, and medical service providers (italics added)."*

Positive Considerations of a White-Collar Crime

1. *It pays well.*
   It has been said that each white-collar crime averages $23,500. Proceeds are "tax free."
2. *It is easy.*
   Because most white-collar crime involves collusion, internal controls are usually only a "nuisance."
   There is no heavy lifting, but lots of time off to enjoy the proceeds.
3. *The risk is currently "acceptable."*
   Potential victims usually "cooperate" by ignoring the threat. Proactive (audit) discovery efforts are rare.
   Only a relatively few fraud schemes are discovered. Of these, it has been determined that 80% are discovered accidentally.
   Relatively few fraud schemes that are discovered result in prosecution or other adverse action.
   For those perpetrators who are successfully prosecuted, the penalties are usually "civilized."

Fraud Pays Well. Unfortunately we cannot tell you precisely how well fraud pays because most fraud has never been discovered. And, when fraud is discovered, it is rare that the perpetrator who is prosecuted is charged with the total proceeds of his or her crime. Prosecutors generally limit charges against those accused to instances where the evidence and details can be clearly demonstrated in court, understood by a jury, and cannot be easily challenged by the defense. In the "Charlie Brown" case previously mentioned, a thief was charged with embezzling approximately $300,000. Postdiscovery audit, however, disclosed that the amount embezzled was closer to $900,000 and could have easily been much higher.

Fraud Is Easy. There was a time, perhaps several decades ago, when the difficulty of committing fraud was considerable. Or so it was believed. Public ethics of that era appeared to rule out the probability that two or more persons would be likely to conspire to commit a crime. Making capital on that belief, internal controls were designed into operating systems to make conspiracy "necessary" to commit fraud and, thereby, it was hoped, to control it. Regardless of previous arguments in favor of providing for the "separation of duties" as a fraud preventive device, however, that day has come and passed. Today more and more fraud audit and investigative experience is demonstrating that most fraud involves a conspiracy of two or more persons, thereby effectively overriding many internal controls and leaving the road clear for the commission of the crime.

The Perpetrator's Fraud Risk Is Acceptable. To rob a bank is usually a very difficult and risky affair. A bank's cash is usually not very accessible, electronic protective systems are formidable, and heavily armed guards pose significant bodily peril to the bank robber. Not so for the fraud perpetrator. Any theft by fraud, by definition, involves stealth and deceit. Violence is never involved. Usually the victim never realizes that he or she has been robbed, and there is little likelihood of bodily harm for the perpetrator.

A risk is present, however, in the possible subsequent discovery of a theft by fraud. Not to worry! Like most humans, fraud victims tend to believe, without really seriously considering the threat, that "it can't happen to them." Or they are placated by the popular but inaccurate belief that their independent auditors are on guard against fraud. Unfortunately for them, neither belief is well founded.

That fraud can happen to anyone, we believe, does not have to be argued. Surely any thinking person realizes that fraud can happen to anyone. However, many businesses that are audited every year by independent accountants assume that their examinations are a reasonable protection from fraud. In fact, a research study performed in 1974 found that 66% of the investing public thought so (Survey: "Public Accounting in Transition" conducted for Arthur Anderson & Co. by the Opinion Research Corporation, p. 48).

Such is not the case, however. Independent auditors decline responsibility for discovering fraud. Nor have internal auditors or criminal investigators been a significant threat to perpetrators—unless, of course, they make a mistake and invite attention. Consider how often it happens that in instances of fraud that has been discovered, it has been discovered accidentally, and not as the result of an intentioned audit search. In fact, a recent study disclosed that only 20% of fraud is discovered by auditors.

Nevertheless, there are significant numbers of cases of fraud that are discovered, by whatever means. Do such discoveries constitute a deterrent? Not really. Most perpetrators, whose naivete is like that of their victims, believe that discovery will not happen to them. Moreover, anyone seriously intending to commit fraud would surely research and evaluate the risk of detection. Were such a person to do so, he or she would know that auditors are not a threat and that most fraud is never discovered. Besides, when fraud is discovered it rarely results in adverse action of any kind, including prosecution. However, many *are* prosecuted. Isn't this a deterrent? Wrong again!

It is our experience that the relatively few perpetrators who are prosecuted are not always convicted of fraud. Those who are convicted often get "civilized" sentences because they are often first offenders and their crimes are nonviolent. Rather than going to the "big house," they are more likely to go to a place like the federal prison located on the Elgin U. S. Air Force Base. Located on the Gulf of Mexico, it is quite pleasant for these perpetrators who must undergo the "ultimate" penalty. Its "walls" are stripes painted on the ground. Jogging prisoners are expected to refrain from going over the painted lines. Conceivably, an absent-minded prisoner could jog right off the base. The prison's environment includes tennis courts, hobby facilities, and tropical plants. If prisoners wish to go to nearby Ft. Walton, Florida, to see a baseball game or attend a Rotary Club meeting, these excursions are possible.

The sentence terms are usually not severe. One man convicted on clear and convincing evidence of embezzling $300,000 was given a one-year prison term, to be served in the federal high-rise prison in Chicago's downtown business area. Much of his term had been satisfied by his pretrial confinement, and after sentence was passed he was allowed to leave the prison on a work release program during the daytime hours of the term he did serve. No appreciable restitution was ever made.

In essence, many perpetrators live very well off victims who never even suspect that they are being drained of resources. It is not un- reasonable to assume that 2% of a business's or institution's gross revenues are being lost to fraud, and that 2% of its employees are involved in fraud. As if they are playing a slot machine that requires no coins, they keep pulling the handle and it keeps paying off, year after year. For many businesses, profits are sufficiently high that they do not miss the 2%.

For the average "conservative" perpetrator, life goes on very well—sometimes indefinitely—without detection. They have the option of terminating their risk at any time, and when they have enough in the kitty (unfortunately there is no comparable retirement program provided for the victim), they can simply stop whatever it is they are doing. In a year or two, any evidence is "history."

IS ANYONE WATCHING THE STORE?

Independent Accountants.   A brief review of a most relevant point made in Chapter 2 (The Auditor's Responsibility For Fraud Detec- tion After Treadway) is an appropriate prelude to this section. It is that two major categories of fraud have particular significance in this book. They are:

- fraud that involves a misstatement of financial statement balances; and,
- fraud that involves transactions which do not distort financial statement balances.

To clearly understand what follows, the distinction is important. Independent accountants do have a responsibility for detecting material misstatements of financial statement balances, whether or not they involve fraud. But, in the second category they do not have a responsibility for fraud discovery, nor do they attempt to discover it.

The reader should also understand that the methodology independent accountants apply to discover fraud in financial statement balances, is not what we refer to as fraud-specific auditing. Rather, their fraud discovery responsibility is discharged by traditional procedures used to verify asset and liability balances, not search for fraud. If the balances cannot be verified, a disparity can subsequently turn out to involve fraud. However, disclosure of evidence of fraud is rarely an audit objective.

It is for at least several decades that independent accountants (CPAs in public practice) have declined responsibility to detect fraud. A problem arises, however, in that the declination is not widely known by persons unfamiliar with the principles and standards that guide the practice of public accounting.

There was a time long ago, around the turn of the century, when auditing for fraud *was* an audit priority. For example, Professor Lawrence R. Dicksee's *Auditing: a Practical Manual For Auditors*, published in London in 1898, stated that the chief objects of an audit were (1) the detection of fraud, and (2) the detection of errors. However, Robert H. Montgomery's classic *Auditing Theory and Practice*, published in 1912,

> signaled a departure from the earlier emphasis of auditors on the detection of fraud and errors to the modern focus on the 'financial condition and earnings of an enterprise' (*Journal of Accountancy*, May 1987, p. 149).

(Montgomery was a generally recognized American authority on auditing, a CPA, lawyer, professor of accounting, and past president of the American Institute of Accountants. Encyclopedic in coverage, for many years his "Auditing Theory and Practice" was an authoritative catalog and indispensable companion to the auditor seeking advice and counsel.)

Fraud discovery audit objectives gradually eroded in years subsequent to 1912, until even Montgomery, in his 1957 edition described the detection of fraud as "a responsibility not assumed."

FRAUD-SPECIFIC AUDITING

In 1978 the Commission on Auditors' Responsibilities (an independent commission established by the American Institute of Certified Public Accountants) Report, Conclusions, and Recommendations attempted to clarify the auditor's responsibilities for detecting fraud. In their report they wrote:

> No major aspect of the independent auditor's role has caused more difficulty for the auditor than questions about his responsibility for the detection of fraud. In the last ten years, a number of major frauds that auditors have failed to detect have focused unfavorable attention on this aspect of the audit function.

Continuing, their report stated that:

> independent auditors have always acknowledged some responsibility to consider the existence of fraud in conducting an audit. Nevertheless, the nature and extent of that responsibility have been unclear. Court decisions, criticisms by the financial press, actions by regulatory bodies, and surveys of users indicate dissatisfaction with the responsibility for fraud detection acknowledged by auditors.
> Opinion surveys in this and other countries indicate that concerned segments of the public expect independent auditors to assume greater responsibility in this area. Significant percentages of those who use and rely on the auditor's work rank the detection of fraud among the most important objectives of an audit."

It is interesting that during the time that auditors were moving away from the detection of fraud as an object of audit and declining a responsibility to detect fraud, those who used the services of auditors were generally unaware of this change. The 1974 survey conducted by the Opinion Research Corporation for Arthur Andersen & Co mentioned earlier indicated that 66% of the investing public believed that

> "the most important function of the public accounting firm's audit of a corporation is to detect fraud."

In 1972 the American Institute of Certified Public Accountants provided the following opinion statement on auditor responsibilities to disclose fraud:

Reliance for the prevention and detection of fraud should be placed principally upon an adequate accounting system with appropriate internal control. . . . If an objective of an independent auditor's examination were the discovery of all fraud, he would have to extend his work to a point where its cost would be prohibitive. Even then he could not give assurance that all types of fraud had been detected, or that none existed, because items such as unrecorded transactions, forgeries, and collusive fraud would not necessarily be uncovered. . . . *It is generally recognized that good internal control and fidelity bonds provide protection more economically and effectively (italics added) (Codification of Auditing Standards and Procedures 1, 110.06).*

The codification was obviously a well-intended effort to allow auditors to adopt a unified position formally declining responsibility for the discovery of fraud, with cogent reasons provided for doing so. However, it can be argued that it settled nothing and in fact further muddled the controversy. For example, in attempting to get auditors "off the hook" for fraud discovery responsibility, the official codification correctly reasoned that to expect the auditor to discover *all* fraud would be unreasonable. This conclusion is valid to this day. However, *it was not a valid reason then, nor is it a valid reason today, for the auditor to set aside and thereby waste his or her excellent qualifications and abandon his or her responsibility to search for fraud,* merely because he or she could not take responsibility to discover *all* fraud.

It is difficult to disagree with *Codification 1* in that accounting and internal controls provide protection against fraud. The *Codification* is deficient, however, in asserting that they can be relied upon to do so. They cannot. There is no substitute for fraud-specific auditing to control fraud.

We have seen attempts to design and implement internal control systems without the benefit of auditing to control fraud. Theoretically, and simplistically, it makes sense to attempt to "close the barn door to prevent the horse from running away." Today, however, it is seldom wise or justifiable to rely upon internal controls and fidelity bonds to prevent fraud or compensate victims of fraud. There are many frauds today that cannot be deterred by internal controls regardless of how comprehensive they may be, and fidelity bonds are only compensatory in those few cases in which frauds are detected and fully evaluated.

Lest there be any confusion on this point, for protection against fraud it is essential that there be (1) a good financial accounting and management reporting system, (2) cost-effective internal control, and (3) fraud-specific auditing. Fidelity bonds do not combat fraud, and no further mention of them will be made here.

Some independent auditors have been outspoken on the issue of their responsibility for discovering fraud. In commenting on "What an audit can do," Robert E. Hanson of Arthur Young & Co. [from a speech in Los Angeles, May 3, 1977] stated:

> The very nature of fraud requires devious means. Most frauds are collusive, and sometimes represent off-the-book transactions. In making his audit, the independent auditor proceeds by examining only a small fraction of a company's transactions. It is highly unlikely that he would come across questionable payments in the course of a normal review of his client's financial records. The alternative—to look at all transactions— would be impossible in terms of time and ridiculous in terms of money. (*Journal of Accountancy*, Dec. 1977)

Currently, the auditor's responsibility for detecting fraud is a rather sensitive subject. Independent auditors see their responsibility as understood by many as synonymous with *liability*. Accordingly, they are understandably reluctant to deal with the issue of responsibility. To them we would recommend problem confrontation, which would involve making it very clear to clients of their services that customary independent audit fees do not include fraud auditing methods, and, hence, those engagements do not accept responsibility for finding fraud. In addition, we would recommend that they make available fraud auditing engagements to their clients which would accept limited responsibility for the disclosure of all significant fraud. Such audit activities would employ fraud auditing field standards and methods, substantially increase the likelihood of significant fraud discovery, and deter fraud by greatly increasing the risk of discovery for the perpetrator.

A recent, April 1988, pronouncement of the AICPA attempts to update and to further clarify the independent auditor's nonresponsibility for discovering fraud, *and even his or her nonresponsibility to look for it.* Paragraph 7 of the *Statement on Auditing Standards (SAS) 54* states that an audit made in accordance with generally accepted auditing standards provides no assurance that illegal acts will be detected or that any contingent liabilities that may result will be disclosed.

Paragraph 8 further asserts that

normally, an audit in accordance with generally accepted auditing standards *does not include audit procedures specifically designed to detect illegal acts (italics added).*

It appears that *SAS 54* continues to err in equating a "responsibility to detect fraud" with "a responsibility to search for fraud." The unfortunate effect is to take the most qualified proactive fraud combatants (the auditors) out of the arena, effectively abandoning it to the perpetrator.

Obviously concerned with the movement away from the detection of fraud as an object of audit, in their 1978 report the Commission of Auditor's Responsibilities (AICPA) recommended that

the prudent auditor will seek knowledge of methods of perpetrating, concealing, and detecting fraud. Conditions indicating fraud and the methods of perpetrating fraud are not always obvious and change as the business environment changes. Auditors should recognize those changing conditions and be knowledgeable about the latest methods of perpetration and detection.

Methods and procedures should be adopted for public accounting firms to exchange information on developments in the perpetration and detection of fraud. *The AICPA should establish means for the regular dissemination of that type of information (italics added).*

The Commission's recommendation was an excellent one, and a worthy attempt to initiate independent auditor training and interest in fraud. However, in 1987 a former official of the AICPA was asked why the Commission's recommendation for CPAs to collect and exchange information on the perpetration and detection of fraud was not successful. He replied simply, "No one chose to share their experiences."

FRAUD-SPECIFIC AUDITING

Internal Auditors.   Undoubtedly there are some internal auditors who are practicing fraud auditing effectively. However, the vast majority of internal auditors are simply not practicing effective fraud auditing, despite their probable protestations to the contrary. To those who might be comfortable in the feeling that they *are* auditing for fraud effectively, it would be well for them to reexamine their reasons for this belief. In doing so, the following questions would be useful:

1. How did you acquire your fraud-specific auditing expertise? Since the practice is a relatively new one, teachers, learning opportunities, and on-the-job experiences are rare.
2. What benchmarks do you use to make conclusions about your effectiveness? That is, what generally accepted methodologies or general and field auditing standards do you use?

If a lesson is to be learned here at all, it is that an auditor can *never* afford to become complacent, regardless of his or her experience or the results of audit being experienced. *There are no expert fraud auditors—yet.* In addition, the auditor should seek out frequent opportunities for competent training to add to his or her fraud discovery sensitivity and skills.

Auditors must immediately begin to accept (1) the responsibility to search for fraud, and the (2) limited responsibility for discovering fraud.

7

FRAUD AUDITING STANDARDS, METHODOLOGY, AND CLASSIFICATIONS

STANDARDS

Perhaps the first problem the fraud auditor or investigator faces in accepting any degree of responsibility for searching for and discovering fraud is the lack of "General Standards for Fraud Auditing and Investigating" (GSFAI), and "Field Standards for Fraud Auditing and Investigating" (FSFAI). Until they are developed it will be difficult for truly professional practice to develop systematically and effectively.

Obviously, there must be generally accepted standards and guidelines that practitioners can reference for the purpose of evaluating the adequacy of fraud audit and investigation procedures, if any degree of responsibility for fraud discovery is to be meaningful.

This part of this book seeks to begin to establish what will, it is hoped, become Generally Accepted Standards for Fraud Auditing and Investigating" (GASFAI). Comments, recommendations, and constructive criticism, would be sincerely appreciated from any reader of this material who would like to participate as a charter member in this effort, and who would like to have an impact on the emerging practice of fraud-specific audits and investigations. Recommendations received will be compiled into an "Exposure Draft" of "General Standards for Fraud Auditing and Investigating" for prepublication comments by all those who have participated. Depending on the comments received, a draft compilation of "Field Standards for Fraud Auditing and Investigating" will be started.

If there is sufficient interest, charter enrollment in the Fraud Auditors and Investigators Association (FAIA) will be offered. There are no limitations on the professional qualifications of those who may seek membership, only a sincere interest in the subject. However, accountants, auditors, investigators, and lawyers, including their counterparts in academia, will in all probability constitute the primary membership.

All persons interested in commenting, becoming charter members, or otherwise wishing to participate in this effort should contact:

> Fraud Auditors and Investigators Association
> 4324 R2 Drectrah Road
> La Crosse, WI 54601

The General Standards discussed below reflect the formative opinions of the FAIA staff. They are a beginning to the difficult task of formulating standards for fraud auditing and investigating. They are subject to possibly many changes in accordance with what will eventually become the "generally accepted views" of the FAIA membership.

On Auditors and Investigators

Before presenting the first draft standards, it is appropriate to respond to anticipated questions about why standards are being designed to apply jointly to the professions of auditing and investigating. As fraud-experienced auditors and investigators are aware, the two professions tend not to work together primarily because their skills and practices differ significantly. Auditors tend to be proactive, to search for indicia of fraud; investigators tend to be reactive, to search for evidence of fraud. Generally, auditors who discover indicia of fraud withdraw from the case, leaving the criminal investigators to seek and compile evidence of the crime. This separation of functions often results in impaired communication, delayed case development, and difficulty in the speedy prosecution of fraud.

Each profession has unique skills, training, and experience that are invaluable to combat fraud, whether the approach be proactive or reactive. The fraud auditor is clearly handicapped when he or she does not have at hand the skills normally possessed by investigators. Likewise, the fraud investigator is clearly handicapped when he or she does not have at hand skills normally possessed by auditors. This fraud combat dichotomy is certainly another of the major reasons that prosecution is declined in so many cases of fraud. The evidence developed for many cases is simply not "good enough" to support prosecution.

To improve fraud combat it is necessary to marry the two professions into a unified effort. Undoubtedly, the day will come when a hybrid profession and professional will emerge to be known by a self-descriptive job title. (You may wish to think of names such as "Fraudigation," "Frauditor," or my favorite, "Fraudigator.")

Accordingly, it is appropriate that any formal beginning to a professional approach to fraud discovery and control should include recognition of the need for common standards to provide for the anticipated joint efforts of auditors and investigators. Additionally, the profession must regain the public trust through standards that instill sound professional conduct of auditors and investigators.

Standards for Fraud Auditing and Investigating

First General Standard for Fraud Auditing and Investigating. The audit/investigation is to be performed by a person or persons having adequate technical training and proficiency in fraud auditing and fraud investigating.

Note: The First General Standard For Fraud Auditing and Investigating was adapted from the First General Standard for independent accountants issued by the American Institute of Certified Public Accountants.

Second General Standard for Fraud Auditing and Investigating. The audit/investigation shall be supplemented by the services of a person or persons having whatever technical or other knowledge which may be necessary to competently assist audit/investigative personnel in documenting suspected fraudulent transactions.

Note: In fraud audits/investigations fraud auditors and investigators frequently find themselves with a need to evaluate specialty areas that require expert knowledge not possessed by the auditors or investigators involved.

Third General Standard for Fraud Auditing and Investigating. In all matters relating to an assignment, an independence in mental attitude is to be maintained by auditor(s) and investigator(s).

Note: The Third General Standard for Fraud Auditing and Investigating is similar to the Second General Standard issued by the AICPA. The Third General Standard was written primarily to apply to the relationship that normally is expected to prevail between independent auditors or private investigators and clients. However, it applies with reasonably equal significance to internal auditors and internal investigators. The internal auditor/investigator *must* have a privileged relationship with a top official or committee of his or her firm, agency, or institution, which allows him or her to function independently in the performance of his or her duties.

Fourth General Standard for Fraud Auditing and Investigating. Due professional care is to be exercised in the performance of the audit/investigation and in specifically and descriptively documenting the suspected fraud.

Note: The Fourth General Standard for Fraud Auditing and Investigating is very similar to the AICPA Third General Standard for independent accountants.

Fifth General Standard for Fraud Auditing and Investigating. The fraud auditor and investigator must not have conflicts of interest, and should scrupulously *avoid* all occasions which could result in a conflict of interests, or even the appearance of a conflict of interests. Appropriate behavior includes declining to conduct an audit or investigation if necessary to avoid such conflict.

Note: The fraud auditor and investigator must avoid personal relationships with the subject(s) of an audit/investigation, or if unavoidable, yield audit/investigative responsibility to another. Also, from time to time the fraud auditor/investigator will very likely be offered gratuities, such as tickets to sporting events, discounts on clothing, various employee privileges, gifts of all sorts, free trips, vacation outings, and similar items of value. Regardless of how innocently or sincerely they are offered, they should be graciously but firmly declined.

Sixth General Standard for Fraud Auditing and Investigating. The fraud auditor and investigator must conduct the audit and investigation in such a manner that it will not bring attention to the facts of fraud prior to completion of the audit and investigation.

Note: (1) The personnel (auditor/investigator) involved must be secretive and protect work notes and products throughout the audit/investigative process. This careful behavior will reduce the inadvertent misplacement or loss of documents and evidence. (2) The discovery of indicia of fraud normally occasions an examination of the activities of one or more suspected perpetrators. This is unavoidable in auditing or investigating fraud. However, all suspects being examined must be given the presumption of innocence, and *exceptional care* must be taken to avoid giving the suspect, *or anyone else*, the impression that he or she is being audited or investigated as a fraud suspect. If necessary, the auditor or investigator must extend the scope of his or her work so as to provide a "cover" for the intentioned fraud examination.

Seventh General Standard for Fraud Auditing and Investigating. The auditor and investigator must *commit* themselves to a referred case of fraud with time, effort, and documentation until the respective employer (client) and prosecutor make a final disposition on it.

Field Standards for Fraud Auditing and Investigating

"Field Standards for Fraud Auditing/Investigating" (FSFAI) have not yet been drafted but will be prepared and issued, as time passes, without limitation, to guide the practice of fraud auditing and investigating. For example, guidance standards will one day surely define the limits of responsibility accepted by fraud auditors and investigators in proactive examinations. Undoubtedly, for example, the FSFAI will provide that the limits of responsibility for discovering fraud will vary with the type of fraud involved and the relative difficulty of discovering it. For example, greater responsibility should ordinarily be accepted for discovering fraud open on-the-books as opposed to fraud that occurs off-the-books.

One last reminder: recommendations from readers are requested, and those received will be carefully considered. The quality of the final product and the general acceptance of the standards that emerge are highly dependent on the quality and quantity of input received from all readers and practitioners in the core professions of accounting, auditing, investigating, and law.

METHODOLOGY

In the view of many people, including auditors, auditing is auditing is auditing, primarily because they have never consciously had reason to think about it. However, as in many professions, there are numerous practice specialties that are so unlike that there are few similarities in audit programs, techniques, and objectives. To mention only a few, there are "independent public accounting" and "internal auditing," two general categories of auditing that are considerably unlike. And within each, there are a myriad of auditing specialities, including bank auditing, insurance auditing, EDP (or ADP) auditing, governmental auditing, contract auditing, operational auditing, compliance auditing, and transportation auditing. The audit process and skills required in each category or specialty are so unique that an auditor adequate in any one would not necessarily be adequate in another.

Fraud auditing is an audit specialty, but currently it has few competent specialists. An attempt to explain the specialty's failure to develop has been included earlier in this chapter. Regardless of the number of its skilled practitioners, however, it is nevertheless an audit specialty, and a brief explanation of its functions will be presented. For language convenience all other audit categories or audit specialties will be referred to as "traditional" auditing.

There are compelling reasons that auditors performing traditional audits are reluctant to accept responsibility for discovering fraud, that is, without significantly increasing their time/cost expenditure. The objectives and the approach methodologies of traditional auditing and fraud auditing have so many fundamental differences that the two audit practices can be said to be incompatible. For example, the independent accountant engaged to perform the customary financial statement opinion examination could not possibly make a competent search for fraud in the same time frame.

In simple terms, in traditional auditing the auditor tends to be primarily concerned with determining the characteristics of an audit universe. More specifically, he or she tends to selectively test representative accounting transactions primarily for the purpose of determining the degree to which internal control and the accounting system is reliable for generating accurate financial statements. During the testing process the auditor's mental attitude is such that he or she expects, and in fact hopes, that the testing is negative. Errors and the like only complicate the audit process. In fact, the traditional auditor's disposition of discrepancies is usually determined by their materiality and the effect they will have on the financial account balances. Discrepancies that do not have a material effect on the financial statements are often only informally reported for corrective action. The objective is not to find fraud, but to determine the reliability of asset/liability account balances which enter into the preparation of financial statements. Fraud disclosure sometimes occurs as a bonus or by- product of traditional audit transaction testing. However, the tests are not designed to detect fraud, and do not effectively do so.

In sharp contrast, the auditor seeking to discover fraud is normally not particularly interested in determining characteristics of the audit universe or whether financial account balances are properly stated. Rather, his or her objective is to discover whether or not fraud is being practiced in the audit universe and to find the individuals responsible for it. Although fraud auditing may involve transaction testing, the transaction selection process is usually biased. Transaction examination is usually more exhaustive in an audit to discover fraud, and immaterial discrepancies or defects are not quickly disregarded but may have evidenciary value as indicia of fraud.

Although both traditional audits and fraud audits examine accounting transactions, there is usually a significant difference in the manner in which transactions are selected for examination. The traditional auditor tends to select transactions on a random basis to eliminate personal bias, so as to allow projection of examination results to characterize the audit universe. Although the fraud auditor also selects accounting transactions to be examined, the selection process is not likely to be made on a random basis, since there is usually no need to project results. Rather, transactions are selected literally in a biased manner which will maximize the likelihood of finding fraud.

To better understand the difference between audit methodologies, an analogy comparing traditional auditing and fraud aUditing to the art of fishing is useful.

Consider, for example, what a traditional auditor might do if he were hired to express an opinion on "How many fish are in Lake Crystal." Note that the objective is not "to catch fish." Following a methodology similar to that which he might ordinarily use in traditional auditing, he would very likely statistically sample the lake, dropping a hook into the water with a grid-like precision which would allow him to cover, without personal bias, all parts of the lake. When finished he would likely be in a position to say with 95% accuracy that there were *no* fish in the lake, give or take a 2 to 3% error. And they would be correct. Although he might have gotten lucky and caught a fish, as he occasionally catches fraud, it is not lilkely. But then, that was not his objective.

Assume, further, that the fraud auditor was also fishing, using techniques similar to those she uses in searching for fraud, during the same days that the traditional auditor was sampling the lake. Rather than dropping a hook in a grid-like pattern over the whole lake, she instead dropped her hook, during the early morning hours, into a cool, shady pool near the north end of Lake Crystal. She selected that spot because she knew that the fish she was searching for abhor bright sunlight and hot water. In total, she might have dropped as many hooks into the water as the traditional auditor fisherman, but her chances of catching fish would have been significantly increased.

There is one additional thing that the expert fisherman would do that should be emulated by fraud auditors. When they detect indicia that fish are present, perhaps by a nibble on their lure, they concentrate all their efforts to coincide with the indicia. Where there are signs that fish are present, fish may be present. Where there is smoke, there may be fire. Where there are indicia of fraud, there may be fraud.

CLASSIFICATIONS OF FRAUD

Can fraud be classified in such a way as to improve its detection? Yes! It can be classified in a number of ways, and, in fact, it *must* be classified if the proactive discovery process is to be reasonably successful, in that *different* procedures are required to discover each type of fraud and to control each type's occurrence. And, of course, the procedures useful in discovering certain specific types of fraud will be less useful or even ineffective in discovering others.

The experienced auditor or investigator does not search for fraud, per se, without having a specific type of fraud in mind, any more than a fisherman goes fishing without having in mind the type of fish he will fish for. Having in mind the specific something that you may be looking for greatly improves your chances of finding it, whether it be fraud or fish. The use of specific tools and techniques makes the difference. For example, the fisherman who decides to go trout fishing takes along equipment and lures that are best suited to catch trout, and travels to a trout stream. Once there, he applies skills suitable only for catching trout. If he changes his mind and decides to fish for bass, his trout gear will be useless. He will have to take along entirely different equipment, plus lures, and will probably get a boat.

Similarly, the fraud auditor must first learn the types of fraud that are most likely to be swimming in her audit lake. She must then decide what specific type to look for. Once a type is selected for her search, she must then decide upon the audit program she will use. If she decides that her client or employer is vulnerable to conspiratorial kickbacks, for example, she must then design testing that is most likely to expose them. Each classification of fraud is best discovered by using specific ways and means.

There are endless possible variations of fraud. And, we couldn't possibly do justice to their description, even if we knew them all. There is a saying among fraud auditors that the "best" fraud schemes remain undiscovered. However, in the paragraphs that follow we will attempt to describe some of the major classifications of fraud that the fraud auditor or investigator uses in programming his or her search for evidence.

Note: Readers desiring further training and exposure to types of fraud and audit/investigative techniques should seek to attend either an Institute of Management Accountants, Professional Education Program (PEP) session of the subject, or a session periodically offered by the Executive Education Series, Inc. If sufficient interest is expressed, a course will be specifically designed to meet the needs and desires of the requesting group.

Before delving into some of the various "garden varieties" of transaction fraud, it is well to note that a major category of transaction fraud, which we will call "specialty" fraud, will be given only brief mention. It is unique to certain industries, and in-depth discussion of the fraud possibilities in any one industry would have little general benefit. They are more appropriately handled in books and courses dedicated to one industry. However, perhaps the largest single category of the specialty frauds is what we prefer to call the "custodial" frauds. Custodial fraud, as the name implies, refers to the embezzlement of assets entrusted by depositors and members to institutions such as banks, savings and loans, credit unions, pension funds, insurance entities, and so forth.

One need only read any news source in 1989 and the early 1990s to be aware of the many abuses of custodial responsibility in the savings and loan industry. At this writing, the taxpayer bailout of ailing savings and loan institutions and banks is estimated to be over $500 billion. To add additional dimension to the reader's understanding of abuses of custodial responsibilities, we have included in Chapter 12 some interesting excerpts from relatively recent Department of Labor Inspector General reports dealing with pension fund abuses and frauds.

Some additional understanding of the intricacies of custodial fraud can be seen in the following grand jury indictment that was handed down in July 1990. S & L No. 1, a Texas association, was charged with offering S & L No. 2, also a Texas association, a $6 million profit on any piece of real property that it wished to dispose of. S & L No. 1, in return asked S & L No. 2 to provide $30 million in financing for certain California properties that it wanted to buy. After selecting the property it wanted to sell, S & L No. 2 lent a buyer (an agent of S & L No. 2) $16.8 million to buy the property from S & L No. 2. S & L. No. 1 then lent the buyer $22.6 million to cover the principal of S & L No. 2's loan, plus interest, and a $6 million profit for S & L No. 2. S & L No. 2 then lent S & L No. 1 $30 million to buy the California properties. Confused? You're not alone. Both S & Ls subsequently failed.

The general classifications of fraud that follow are neither all inclusive nor mutually exclusive. It will soon become apparent to the reader that many types of fraud will fall into at least two noncontradictory classifications.

Three Basic Categories of Fraud

Three basic categories into which fraud can be classified include the theft of assets which

1. Appears openly on the books as distinct accounting entries;
2. Appears on the books, but is hidden as a part of other larger otherwise legitimate accounting entries; and
3. Is not on the books, and could never be detected by an examination of "booked" accounting transactions.

The order in which these categories are listed indicates the relative difficulty of discovering them—from least difficult to discover to most difficult to discover.

Fraud Open on-the-Books.   Relatively speaking, open fraud is the easiest to discover. It includes those criminal acts that involve discrete entries in the accounting records. In using the term *discrete entry* we mean that the fraud involves the entire transaction, which if selected by an auditor for examination, offers the best chance for discovery.

A fraudulent duplicate payment of $500 to a vendor is an example. The $500 item would appear in the accounting records as a $500 transaction, most probably in a check register or accounts payable register. If selected by an auditor for review, it would have to "stand by itself," and a careful examination of supporting documentation and related particulars would very probably disclose the duplicate payment.

Fraud Hidden on-the-Books.   As the name suggests, hidden fraud involves acts of fraud that are included in accounting entries which appear on the books, but they are not discrete entries. That is, the amount of the fraud is always buried in a larger legitimate accounting entry, and never appears as a discrete amount. Accordingly, an auditor can select the host entry for examination and verify that it is legitimate, yet never detect the fraud.

An example of hidden fraud is the kickback. For example, a $50,000 purchase of factory raw materials could be overpriced to provide a $5000 kickback to an employee who was influential in purchasing the raw materials at the excessive price. A $90,000 contract for installing a security system might be overpriced to provide for a $9000 kickback to an employee who steered the business to the company doing the work. Unless the auditor is sensitive to what things should cost, he or she will never detect the fraud, even though a thorough review of supporting documentation is made. The experienced fraud auditor looking for kickbacks (remember the fishing story?) may not look at any transaction documentation. But he or she may go directly to an examination of unit prices charged to attempt to determine their reasonableness.

A further illustration is the actual case of an auditor in New York City who was examining purchases of office equipment made by his employer over a span of time. He noticed that a certain brand of dictating machine appeared to be overpriced. Hundreds of the machines had been purchased at a price of about $300 each. During his lunch hour, he walked down the street to a small office supply store. There he examined one of the machines and determined that it was identical to those he was auditing. He then asked the merchant the price at which he could purchase one of the machines. The merchant quoted a price of $225.

The variety of fraud that is hidden-on-the-books is endless. It constitutes by far the largest category of fraud. It is often difficult to find and requires particular resourcefulness on the part of the auditor, such as in our New York example.

Another hidden fraud might be the substitution of less expensive materials than those ordered and paid for. The fraud is usually accompanied by an inside conspirator who assures acceptance of the materials. For example, a payment of $75,000 to seal the roof of a warehouse with a high-quality expensive Brand X waterproof coating might have had a cheaper Brand Y substituted, which was worth $50,000. Detection by the average auditor is difficult. At this point, it is useful to review the draft "Second General Standard for Fraud Auditing and Investigating" included earlier in this chapter. Briefly, it provides that

> the audit/investigation shall be supplemented by the services of a person or persons having whatever technical or other knowledge which may be necessary to competently assist audit/investigative personnel.

In this instance, the fraud auditor might well feel it necessary to request the assistance of someone who could test the roof material to assure that Brand X had in fact been applied.

The only way a fraud auditor has of detecting kickbacks and/or the substitution of lower-quality materials, is to be very knowledgeable of competitive prices and other particulars of products and services being purchased. This is a degree of competence not required of traditional auditors. When searching for kickbacks the auditor must *attempt to determine that the price is not excessive, and that the buyer received what was bargained for.* Any excessive pricing or sacrifice in product quality or quantity should be immediately suspected as indicia of fraud.

Of course, sometimes auditors just get lucky in looking for kickbacks. One auditor found a notation on a vendor's invoice that said, "Deliver color TV set to Mr. Jones, 616 N. Elm Street."

Fraud off-the-Books. In fraud off-the-books, as the name suggests, the amount of the fraud is never a discrete accounting entry, and is never a hidden part of an accounting entry. Perhaps the best way to describe the most common fraud off-the-books, is that for the victim it is the loss of a valuable entitlement. For example, an entity may be entitled to receive a share of the proceeds from vending machines, cafeteria operations, sales of scrap materials, and so forth. However, the revenues are "diverted" by a thief.

Another example might be the conversion of payments on accounts receivable which have been written off. Obviously, if the fraud involves diverting those proceeds, the victim has lost unrecorded assets. Obviously, too, no amount of auditing book transactions is likely to disclose the diversion. Discovery techniques require the auditor to speculate on existing unrecorded assets that might be the objects of fraud, and then to initiate appropriate audit testing designed to disclose whether or not fraud has actually occurred.

Nonrepeating and Repeating Fraud

All frauds can be classified as being nonrepeating (or one-time fraud) or repeating fraud which, having been triggered once, occurs again and again.

Nonrepeating Fraud. In nonrepeating fraud, a fraudulent act, even though repeated many times, is singular in nature in that it must be triggered by the perpetrator each time. And, each time it is triggered, somewhere there is documentation or other evidence of the initiating act that offers an opportunity for discovery. Each act of fraud is a separate act of fraud.

An example is a fraudulent payroll check issued each week to the perpetrator, provided that the payroll system is a "positive" system that requires an input such as a time card every week to generate the fraudulent paycheck. The perpetrator must therefore generate a new fraudulent time card every week. Every week a new act of fraud is committed, even though the deception may go on for a prolonged period of time.

Repeating Fraud. In repeating fraud, a defrauding act may occur many times; however, it needs to be initiated only once. It then keeps running until it is stopped. It could possibly recur in perpetuity. An example might be found in a payroll situation in which a salaried employee gets the same salary every two weeks—provided the payroll system is a "negative" system. A negative system is so called because it requires "negative" input to keep functioning once it has been started. Once begun the system will generate a payment to whoever is designated, in perpetuity, until a stop order is issued. Negative systems are not unusual where certain salary payments remain the same for a reasonably long period. An annuity payment system might also be negative based, such as the government's Social Security system. The negative system is a convenience since it eliminates the need to keep initiating input for each period. When a negative system is used by a perpetrator to generate a payroll check for a fictitious employee, for example, the checks will be issued each period without his further input. Although the fraud could conceivably repeat many times, it is nevertheless, *one* act of fraud.

The variety of repeating frauds is limited only by the creativity of the perpetrator, and some of them are very creative. In one instance a bank computer programmer had adjusted a computer program to skim a few cents off every customer's account service charge. No customers ever complained, because the loss for any one account was miniscule and the service charge computation so complicated. With average daily account balances entering into the computation formula, verification was all but impossible. The fraud, which accumulated a few cents from many customers, produced sizable cumulative revenues for the perpetrator without any monthly action required on her part to initiate the fraud. Discovery was most accidental.

For the fraud auditor, the significance of whether a fraud is non-repeating or repeating lies in where he or she will look for the evidence. In the bank fraud illustration given, a minute review of the computer program would probably have offered the only reasonable clue. However, the auditor would have had to have a good working knowledge of computer programming and a lot of patience.

Fraud and Conspiracy

Obviously, fraud can be classified as that which involves conspiracy and that which does not involve conspiracy. However, there is a third category which is too often ignored by auditors. It is fraud which involves "pseudo" conspiracy.

In a fraud scheme which involves a pseudo conspiracy, two or more persons act together to defeat existing internal controls. What makes it different from conspiracy is that one or more of the parties to the fraud is innocent of fraudulent intent. Often they do not realize the significance of the internal control they are responsible for administering, or they are just plain negligent.

Some readers may be uncomfortable using the term conspiracy rather than "collusion," a term it seems is preferred by many accountants. According to the *American Heritage Dictionary* (Second College Edition, 1985), conspiracy is described as "An agreement to perform an illegal, treacherous, or evil act," and collusion is described as "A secret agreement between two or more persons for a deceitful or fraudulent purpose."

To many auditors and accountants the word *collusion* is preferred. We believe, however, that there is little if any difference in meaning when used by accountants and auditors, and they will be used synonymously in these chapters. We prefer to use *conspiracy* because of its specific usage in law. And, we believe that indicia of fraud must always be pursued with an expectation that prosectuion and the courts will become involved.

Collusion in fraud schemes has become common. At one time it was generally accepted that internal controls which provided for a separation of duties may fraud a remote possibility. Conventional wisdom was that although one person might contemplate fraud, it was extremely unlikely that two or more persons would conspire in a fraudulent act. It was believed that they would be extremely reluctant to expose their criminal intent to another, or to trust another person with knowledge that could convict them of a crime.

It would be pointless to attempt to discover if that conventional wisdom was ever valid, because current experience discloses that most fraud involves conspiracy, either bona fide or pseudo. And it is becoming particularly brazen. In one instance, an office supply broker would visit store managers, explain "how to commit fraud," and offer to facilitate and participate in it. As a broker of office supplies, such as ball-point pens, he would accept a purchase order for a large quantity of pens and provide the store manager with the customary shipping documents and invoices for pens ordered—but never ship them. The store manager would then process the documents for payment, certifying receipt, and later share the payment with his broker "conspirator." Although many office supply stores were involved, no one turned in the friendly broker.

Intentional or, often, unwitting conspiracy is involved in almost every fraud, and is usually necessary to execute the fraud. Most fraud victims, or victims-in-waiting (everyone is a victim-in-waiting), have internal controls that deter fraud committed by perpetrators acting alone. The term *victim-in-waiting* is derived from an old pilot's saying: "There are only two kinds of pilots flying retractable landing gear airplanes: those who have landed with their wheels up, and those who someday will."

Thus, there are only two kinds of entities, those that have been fraud victims, and those that someday will be fraud victims.

Accordingly, fraud auditing must consider the likelihood of conspiracy and perform audit testing as though there were conspiracy. *Pseudoconspiracy* may appear to be a contradiction in terms. In coining and using it, we mean that one party to the conspiracy has criminal intent. The other party does not, but by virtue of his or her innocent cooperation with the criminal, becomes a de facto conspirator in that his or her involvement is necessary to override one or more internal controls. Without the unwitting cooperation of this second party, the fraud may not be possible.

A previous example included just such an unwitting conspiracy. A fraud perpetrator who embezzled over $900,000 by submitting fictitious invoices for building maintenance services required help in his fraud scheme. Before he could enter his fictitious documents into the automated payment system, an accounting control number was required. The processing computer was programmed to allow only documents bearing authorized numbers to be processed, and to assure that all ascending numbers were used, that no transactions were lost, and that no numbers were used twice. The issuance of numbers was controlled by an accounting clerk, who should have issued them only to authorized persons.

However, the perpetrator in this case was well liked by everyone, and the accounting clerk was an innocent young woman who did not realize the important control significance in issuing accounting numbers. When "Mr. Friendly" would occasionally request a block of numbers, she did not think twice about giving them to him. After all, he was an accounting supervisor. And in giving him the control numbers, she became a pseudoconspirator.

It would be difficult to charge her with fraud, however, since she clearly had no intent to defraud, nor did she profit from the fraud. She was however, guilty of negligence, and disciplinary action was warranted.

In the early stages of any search for fraud, or for any systems accountant considering appropriate internal controls, it is somewhat irrelevant whether or not there is agreement between the parties to a fraud. What is important is that two or more parties are likely to be involved in fraud, even though one or more may be innocent parties to it. Innocent or not, they make the fraud possible by allowing internal controls designed to separate responsibilities to be overridden.

There was a time, perhaps a decade or more ago, when accountants designing data processing systems, manual or automated, relied heavily on the unlikelyhood that people would conspire in a fraud scheme. Today, we no longer rely on it. Fraud auditors must recognize the likelihood, and design audit tests accordingly.

Nevertheless, it is still *advisable* that accounting and other administrative systems be designed to include what we generally describe as reasonable "separation of duties." Such an internal control renders fraud more difficult by making collusion necessary to the commission of fraud. However, experience discloses that collusion in fraud is more likely to occur today than it was in the past. Accordingly, less dependence should be placed on separation of duties to deter fraud. We recommend that such controls be supplemented with nondiscretionary internal audit procedures that periodically test to determine that the internal controls are working as designed, and to assure that they are not being circumvented by collusion.

Varieties of Fraud

There are infinite variations of fraud, limited only by the creativity of the perpetrators. And, in the past at least, perpetrators have shown great creativity.

The varieties of fraud can be grouped in two categories: (1) "specialized" fraud, which is unique to certain kinds of business operations, and which only those persons involved with those industries are likely to encounter, and (2) the "garden varieties" of fraud which all people are likely to encounter in general business operations.

Specialized Fraud. Volumes could be written about specialized fraud and still not do it justice. However, what we term as specialized fraud generally refers to those frauds that involve the program funds, or other assets, of specialized industries. Insurance companies and custodial funds, such as pension funds, savings and loans, and the banking industry in general, are typical examples.

For vivid examples, one need only recall the costly scandals involving the savings and loan association failures disclosed in the late 1980s, which resulted in losses of upwards of $500 billion to U. S. taxpayers. Inflated real property appraisals underlying loans and kickbacks to regulators were only a small part of the horror story.

The pillaging of employee pension funds appear to be examples of a current emerging fraud. Relevant and interesting excerpts from a Department of Labor, Inspector General Report for the period ending March 31, 1990, are included in Chapter 12.

Insurance companies in general are particularly in jeopardy from false claims of every sort. Health insurers, for example, are now on guard against false claims involving conspiracies between claimants and company claim processors. Companies paying monthly annuities to beneficiaries are at risk from illegitimate payees inserted into the volumes of checks issued each month. Even the IRS is not immunized against specialized fraud. About 15 years or so ago, prior to the current IRS computer upgrades, the IRS discovered that certain persons were filing false income tax returns claiming refunds of taxes withheld, that were never withheld at all. At the time the IRS, to expedite refunds, was not checking to determine that the withholdings claimed were bonafide. Delivered to apartment house mailboxes, the checks were harvested by perpetrators, long gone when the IRS discovered the frauds.

An example of the lengths to which perpetrators will sometimes go in carrying out a fraud, is one that involved the U.S. Treasury. It occurred about 15 years ago and involved the old machine readable "punched card" Treasury checks that were once in use. At the time, the Treasury did not individually reconcile checks that had been cashed and returned by banks. Rather, they used daily "batch" systems that kept a running account of the total dollar amount of checks issued for each day, as well as the total amount of checks redeemed for each day. Obviously, the aggregate amount of checks redeemed should never exceed the amount issued.

As redeemed checks were returned to the Treasury by Federal Reserve Banks, they would be read by machines that would sort them by day of issue and record the amount of each check. Listings of the checks would be printed, and amounts totaled and reconciled to the "paid" amounts claimed by the redeeming banks. There seldom was a problem in balancing out. However, one day a Treasury worker noticed that for certain days the department had redeemed more dollars than the total amount of checks they had issued. At first there was no alarm, because with the millions of checks involved it was easy to get days mixed up. Reviews of the check listings, however, failed to disclose any obvious errors until eventually, after much hard work, it was discovered that a number of checks issued to Japanese payees had been "raised." That is, with great care and artistry, the payees had increased the amounts of the checks and had received payment for the increased amounts. Their particular creativity became evident when Treasury auditors began to wonder how it was that the fraud was not discovered when the daily reconciliations were made. That is, although the amount of a check could be raised on its face, Treasury accounting machines would still read the "issued" amount from the holes punched into the card stock, and the discrepancy would become evident.

As Paul Harvey might say, the "rest of the story" disclosed extremely clever perpetrators who were apparently aware of the Treasury reconciliation process. To buy themselves a few extra months of time to allow the investigative trail to grow cold, they painstakingly filled the tiny amount holes that the Treasury had punched into the checks when they were issued, and then repunched the checks. This allowed them to "reconcile" as they were redeemed.

Garden Varieties of Fraud. In searching for fraud, as has been previously discussed, it is more productive to search for a specific variety of fraud. There are eight "garden varieties" of fraud, which encompass much of the more common fraud that occurs today. The labels assigned to them are generally descriptive of what is involved:

- Kickbacks.
- Defective pricing.
- Unbalanced contracts or purchase orders.
- Reopening competed contracts.
- Duplicate payments.
- Double payments.
- Shell payments.
- Defective delivery.

1. *Kickbacks.* We prefer to classify kickbacks in at least two groups, kickback I and kickback II.

Most people are familiar with kickback I. A vendor "offers" an *unsolicited* gratuity to a purchasing agent, for example, and the purchasing agent understands an obligation to order a product or service from the vendor. The purchasing agent is often not overconcerned with getting the best price on the merchandise or services he or she buys. There is usually no clear conspiracy between the two parties, in that one never says to the other, "I will give you this in return for that." However, there is usually a tacit conspiracy involved. The wise vendor knows that by withholding the gratuity, many purchasing agents, for example, will withhold ordering from him. The real test might be for the purchasing agent to see how long the vendor keeps offering gratuities with no orders in return. Although many purchasing agents, and like persons with purchasing authority or influence, prefer to recognize the interchange as a standard "acceptable" business practice, both are parties to fraud, unless of course their employer expressly condones it. Employers who condone kickbacks, without reasonable limitations, are asking for trouble. And, the employer may imply his approval of the practice by simply failing to provide "standards of conduct" which stipulate what gratuities his employees may or may not accept. The size of individual or aggregate gratuities can become quite substantial.

Consider the case of the general freight agent for a national railroad who always regretted the second Wednesday of every month. On that day he was expected to visit a major manufacturing plant in the Chicago area to take the entire freight traffic department out for a gala lunch and cocktails. In fact, the department was so large that the luncheon had to be conducted in two shifts. The first shift always left on schedule at 11 A.M., and the second shift was ready to go when the first shift returned. Although the monthly gala was never solicited per se, the railroad's traffic studies showed a significant loss of product tonnage shipped in the month following a "missed" date.

A question here is perhaps, "Who is the instigator?" Is this a conspiracy? Did the two parties come to an agreement—"If you entertain us, we'll use your railroad"? Clearly a subtle form of extortion is involved. However, the gala was always very costly, and all costs were eventually borne by the shipping companies. The unfortunate freight agent acquired bleeding ulcers and died at an early age.

In kickback II, conspiracy is always clearly involved. Either party to the crime may initiate it, but in kickback II both parties agree to a quid pro quo, which provides that "in return for this I will do that." Kickback II tends to work best for products or services that are not mass produced and sold off-the-shelf, and for which there is no customary price. Commercial leased space and janitorial services are just two examples where kickback II fraud works well.

For instance, who can say with any degree of certainty what it should cost to clean the office space at 226 Main Street? Conceivably, the costs could run anywhere from $1.25 a square foot to perhaps $1.75. If 100,000 square feet are involved, for example, a kickback II conspirator could easily increase his or her employer's janitorial costs by $25,000 to $50,000 a year. Similarly, if that 100,000 square feet of office space is being leased, who (in some markets) is likely to question that a lease contract was perhaps increased by $5 a foot, to $30 a square foot, to allow the conspirators to split a windfall of $500,000, particularly when many surrounding properties are being leased for $30 a square foot?

An interesting article appeared in the November 23, 1988, *Wall Street Journal* describing travel agent kickbacks resulting from their choice of, for example, one airline over another. The following are pertinent quotes from the article:

> A survey by Louis Harris & Associates Inc. found that 24% of agents usually use overrides in choosing a carrier. . . . Fears over how this affects service have prompted a growing number of companies to hire auditors to check on travel agencies. One auditing company, Topaz Enterprises of Portland, Ore., says the biggest mistake by agencies it audits is booking one airline when another has a cheaper fare. The average cost of that mistake: $113. One of the reasons: commission overrides.
>
> If I go to an agent and ask for his or her unbiased opinion between cruise ships for me, it's important to know whether the agent is working toward a fur coat" (Ed Perkins, editor of the *Consumer Reports Travel Letter*).

Travel agents who select one airline over another, or one car rental company over another, in return for gratuities, at the expense of travel clients, are participants in kickback II fraud. The quid pro quo is clearly involved.

Kickbacks realized by conspiring insiders may range from insignificant gratuities, such as periodic luncheon parties, to property or cash in significant amounts. Interestingly, where quid pro quos of insignificant amounts are involved, most inside conspirators would argue that a quid pro quo was not involved, that the victim lost nothing because the gratuity received did not influence their purchase judgments. Of course, it is interesting to note that these same people would argue that vendors enjoy spending their money to entertain potential customers without expecting anything in return, and would have you believe that there "really is a tooth fairy."

It is usually not too difficult for a victim to determine whether or not his employees are involved in kickback I. The gratuities are usually openly given and, sad to say, to a degree *have* become industry practice. All employers who allow the practice, should at the very least define limits as to what will be allowed. If they do not, the gratuities can easily escalate to expensive gifts and raise conflicts of interests for their employees. Actual gratuities have ranged from simple luncheons, to the providing of prostitutes, television sets, trips to Europe, and even title to mountain vacation homes.

Kickbacks II are much more difficult for victims or their agents to identify. The events usually involve conspiracy and are not openly known to potential victims. Identification of the transactions and the quid pro quos usually requires fraud-experienced accountants, auditors, or investigators. Perhaps among the most infamous of kickback II examples is the "revolving door" that exists between influential armed forces procurement officers and defense contractors. In awarding "sweetheart" defense contracts or contract decisions to defense contractors, quid pro quos are seldom exchanged on the spot. However, it is general knowledge that those same defense contractors have an open door policy toward hiring those same defense procurement officers when they retire from military service. Is a quid pro quo involved? It would be very difficult to prove. However, we have been in defense contractor plants and have seen rooms full of retired military personnel who were hired ostensibly for their defense experience, but who had few if any job responsibilities.

We believe that nothing in life is free. All gratuities are derived from the donor's profits, and none are given without expecting something in return. Accordingly, we recommend that all entities establish a policy of no gratuities, from anyone, and make it known to all employees that infractions will lead to disciplinary action or prosecution for fraud.

2. *Defective Pricing Fraud.* Defective pricing fraud may often also involve kickback II fraud, but not necessarily. A wide spectrum of fraudulent actions can fall under this one classification. Basically, as the name implies, it involves a pricing defect. When practiced, it results in the victim receiving the full amount and quality of product or service that he bargained for, but ends up paying more than he agreed to.

One clear example of a defective pricing fraud that we recall involved an open contract that called for the provision of various building maintenance services as they might be required throughout the year. The contract provided that the services would be delivered upon demand, and that the cost of the services delivered would be priced at the contractor's prevailing advertised rate, less a 25 percent discount.

Subsequently, an alert auditor performing a routine test of transactions discovered that the contractor had been paid for services delivered, at his prevailing advertised rate, but that he had failed to reduce his invoice by the 25 percent discount agreed upon.

It would be interesting at this point to learn the views of those of you who are reading this. That is, do you feel that the omission was an honest mistake? Or, do you believe that the invoice was intentionally mispriced?

Actually, it is difficult to conclude either way, at this point! It has been our experience that many auditors will conclude that it is an honest mistake. They will report it as such, and recommend recovery of the excessive price charged and paid. In the first encounter we experienced, this is exactly what happened, and about $10,000 was quickly refunded by the contractor involved.

The auditor who has been sensitized to the possibility of fraud being present, however, will usually react differently. He or she might be likely to look upon the finding as a possible indication of fraud. No reporting of the finding would be made, and no recovery of the overpayment recommended. Instead, assuming that the finding may involve fraud, the auditor would be likely to initiate retroactive reviews to determine if the same sort of thing has happened before, noting particularly the contractor involved, and the key employees of the victim that are involved.

The fraud auditor would proceed on the basis that if fraud is involved, it is likely that it has happened before, and that conspiracy is also involved. The conventional wisdom here is that a thief will steal again and again, and if the overcharging has occurred more than once it is almost certain that an inside conspirator would have to be involved to approve payment of the excessive prices charged.

As a matter of fact, even if somehow the auditor was certain that fraud was present, without additional examples of fraud by the contractor or employee involved, it would be virtually impossible to sustain allegations of fraud. It would go down as a mistake. The employee might be found negligent, but would not be found to be a conspirator to fraud.

Auditors who might be engaged in reviewing payment transactions are always advised to learn what pricing provisions the contracts or purchase orders provide for.

3. *Unbalanced Contracts.* Unbalanced contracts are an ideal mechanism for facilitating fraud. They are quite common in interbusiness relationships, and most of them are likely to be bona fide. However, because they facilitate fraud, and because they are in somewhat common legitimate usage, they are always a significant threat to the contracting entity involved. At the time of their issue, it is very difficult to determine the presence of fraudulent intent with any degree of certainty.

An unbalanced contract is one that involves an agreement to deliver multiple products or services, often over a period of time. However, their characteristics that make fraud possible are the individual pricing of the line items to be delivered and the ability of someone to delete or vary the delivery of individual contract line items.

In its simplest version, a contractor with fraudulent intent will usually propose a low total price bid for a contract, in response to a request for bids, which is likely to be under his actual cost, to assure that he is the successful low bidder. However, he will unbalance his bid in such a way that some of the items to be delivered are overpriced, and other items sufficiently underpriced to result in a low aggregate bid. Often it will be the items that are to be delivered first that are overpriced. The perpetrator's strategy is that he or she will not have to deliver on the underpriced items, yielding a handsome profit on the overpriced items that he or she *has* delivered.

As a simple illustration, let us assume that a company requests bids for two things that have to be fabricated, Item A and Item B. Let us further assume that the items should normally cost about $10,000 apiece. Five bidders submit bids to deliver Item A and Item B which range within a few dollars of $20,000. A sixth bidder submits a low bid of $19,000, and he is given the contract.

If you were the company requesting the bids, would you be content with the contract? Ordinarily you should be satisfied that out of six bidders offering prices in the $19,000 to $20,000 range, you have the lowest price. Is there fraud here? In our particular illustration where we control "the facts" there is intent to defraud you, but you haven't lost any money—yet.

A closer examination of the prices that were offered for Item A, however, would show that your contractor offered to fabricate it for $13,000. He offered to fabricate Item B for $6,000. In its simplest form we have here an unbalanced contract. Consider what would happen if delivery of Item B were canceled? The contractor would make a bundle.

Usually, where there is an unbalanced contract, and there is intent to defraud present, the contractor has good reason to depend upon his *not having to deliver* the underpriced items, such as item B.

When unbalanced contracts are used to defraud entities, obviously, they are never as simple as the foregoing illustration. However, the devious formula is always the same. To make the fraud work there is almost always a conspirator who is working for the intended victim, in a capacity in which he or she can influence contract performance. Or the conspirator has privileged information of the sort that the Item Bs of unbalanced contracts are not likely to be required.

Unbalanced contracts can take many forms. Almost always it will not be as simple to notice the unbalanced nature of the contract described in the Item A and Item B example. For example, assume that Item A and Item B were very dissimilar. Assume also that our contractor perpetrator overpriced Item A by $5000, bidding $45,000 to fabricate it, and that he bid $83,850 to fabricate Item B, which should have cost $90,000. Or assume that there were 25 items that were called for in the request for bids. Assume also that the "price spread" between those bid by the perpetrator and the other bidders was not so large as to attract immediate attention. Remember that many legitimate contractors unbalance their bids for very appropriate reasons. Many costs are properly required at the start of production, thereby giving the appearance of a fraudulently unbalanced contract.

Entities should be wary that the lowest price offered to them is not always the best price. There is great difficulty in recognizing unbalanced contracts as having fraudulent intent. For example, a mere inspection of the unit price disparities tells an entity nothing, except to be careful. It is important to keep unbalanced contracts in mind when reading the next part of this chapter on "reopening contracts." There could be a connection.

In the illustrative cases provided for consideration at the end of this chapter, note especially that which involves interior painting. This is a different sort of unbalanced contract that is quite common.

The unbalanced contract scheme is sometimes called *front-end loading*. We prefer *unbalanced contract* because the scheme has more applications than front-end loading.

4. *Reopening Competed Contracts.* Special attention should always be given to contracts that are changed for any of what appear to be urgent and cogent reasons. A "planned" reopening of an advertised contract, for example, is a favored way of steering an advertised contract award to a conspiring contractor. Simply said, the contractor bids a loss price and gets the award, the contract is subsequently reopened for what appear to be valid reasons, and the opportunity is provided to pick the victim's pockets in a wide variety of ways.

This type of fraud is a particularly popular one in businesses, governmental entities, not-for-profit entities, and public institutions, which are normally required to award contracts on the basis of the lowest competitive bid received. Most people presume that the competitive award process assures the lowest price (provided by the marketplace) and protection from fraud, and that they preclude favoritism in selecting a performing contractor. This is not necessarily so.

Where fraud is involved, the process works quite simply and almost always includes a conspirator on the inside.

It could very well happen in this manner. Company A decides to build a warehouse estimated to cost around $1,000,000. Cost proposals are requested from all interested contractors, and their bids are received. Contractor Z is the low bidder, and he receives the contract award to construct the building. After construction is under way, it is discovered that the entrance is not wide enough to admit the type of pallet that will have to pass through. The contract will have to be changed to make the entrance wider. The contract specifications and price are renegotiated to provide for the changes. In addition, the contractor will have to be allowed to recoup his costs expended relative to installing the door required by the original contract, his costs of removing the door, his overhead relative thereto, and so on. Since fraud is involved in our example, it was most certainly planned from the start that the door would have to be changed, and no work or materials were expended to install the original door. Hence, any costs recovered for removing it are without basis, but are pure profit for the conspirators. Of course, the inside conspirator would confirm that the costs claimed were legitimate and necessary.

Again, this illustrative example is intentionally simple to convey how advertised contracts are manipulated to commit fraud. In actual practice, the details get much more involved and may be much less clear. In essence, however, they work the same way.

The federal government is a victim of fraud of this type on a recurring basis. Its contracts are almost always advertised "to assure equal opportunity and fair prices." It hardly ever works that way, however. It is a rare instance when a government contract is not "reopened" for seemingly valid reasons. These are contracts for sophisticated weapons systems, buildings, communications systems, vehicles, office furniture, and almost any other conceivable product.

A particularly flagrant abuse once occurred when the government contracted for the production of metal filing cabinets, to be built to the government's unique specifications. It was expected that the order would total about $14 million. Shortly after the contract was awarded, a government contract representative decided that a change in the cabinet drawer roller mechanism was necessary. The contract was adjusted to require the change specified, and the producer was allowed to claim any necessary costs incidental to the change. The producer claimed and received about $8 million. Audit and engineering studies estimated that the change should not have exceeded $2.5 million.

The U.S. Defense Department is almost never involved in competitive procurement that is not subsequently negotiated to allow for product specification changes. In this way its contracts can be advertised for all to participate and yet steered to a conspiring producer.

As with other commonly used fraud mechanisms, there are countless variations of the reopened contract fraud.

5. Duplicate Payments. This is a very common fraud, simple in concept, that has been around for a long time. It still works. Basically, it is paying a vendor's invoice twice. It usually involves collusion within the victim's office. It may involve collusion with someone in the payee's office. It may not require collusion at all, depending on the victim's internal control system. This type of fraud is always easier with collusion, however. It occurs when an employee of the victim processes an invoice for payment twice. The second payment is intercepted and cashed.

Such fraud is frequently missed by auditors who do not do a thorough job of specifically looking for a duplicate payment (remember the art of fishing?). If an examination is performed at all, an auditor ordinarily will examine the underlying purchase order, find that it is authentic and bears all necessary and appropriate signatures, and so forth. After examining receiving reports that attest to receipt of the product or service that has been paid for, the auditor is likely to "pass" the transaction. A computer-assisted review of all payments made to a selected vendor is probably the best way of detecting duplicate payments.

Relatively speaking, the difficulty of discovering duplicate payment fraud is ranked 1 on a scale of 1 to 10, 1 being easy and 10 being difficult. The fraud is open on-the-books, just sitting there waiting to be found.

6. *Double Payments.* This variety of fraud is related to the duplicate payment. There is, however, a significant difference that is especially important in the discovery process.

In the double payment fraud, an original payment is made to a contractor or vendor for a service or product provided or delivered. For example, $5000 is paid to the Bates Company for remodeling a portion of Building A. There is no fraud involved, and no duplicate payments are made to Bates.

There is fraud present, however, when the perpetrator initiates the necessary paperwork for the Acme Company to be paid $4900 for remodeling the same area of Building A. Acme has done nothing to earn the payment.

The auditor who might choose to examine either transaction separately is not likely to find indicia of fraud. And the selection of both transactions for examination is not likely. Either transaction will have all of the customary supporting documentation intact. The auditor who may choose to go the extra yard and visit the remodeled area to inspect the work will find that it has been done in a perfectly acceptable manner.

The auditor looking for a double payment fraud, however, is likely to find the deception. She may choose to (1) look at project files, if they are properly maintained, and possibly find that two projects were recorded, (2) scan the account (transactions) used to record remodeling projects, and notice suspiciously similar transactions, and (3) when visiting the work site, attempt to determine from people working in the area the identity of the company that did the work. They are likely to tell her that the Bates Company did the work.

This is an example of an open on-the-books fraud, a one-time fraud, which usually involves collusion. The Acme Company is likely to be a conspirator.

7. Shell Payments.   The shell payment is quite similar to the double payment in that a transaction is documented and a payment made, but for a fictitious project. There will be no duplicate payment found, no matter how thoroughly the auditor searches for one, and there will be no double payment found, should the auditor search for one. The project simply does not exist; however, verification is difficult. Such fraud may involve, for example, a $4985 payment to the Brown Company for installing a dedicated 220 volt electric service line to the paint shop. Just as in all legitimate payments, all the paperwork is in order: purchase orders properly authorized, receiving reports properly certified, and invoices properly approved. It may be a bit difficult to verify that the electric line was in fact installed. Such lines are not usually visible. One fraud auditor once told us about a $40,000 payment that he suspected may have been a shell payment. It involved alterations to a building—that was subsequently demolished.

One of two scenarios are likely in shell payments: (1) all the signatures are forged, or, more likely, (2) Gus Baker, the plant electrician, has conspired with the Brown Company to "install" the fictitious electric line, and will defend the need for the line and the Brown Company's work.

Given the facts in the various cases presented in this chapter, it is relatively easy for a reader to say something like, "Oh well, in the shell payment illustration I would have an independent technician crawl up into the ceiling to verify that the electric line was installed." And, if he were to do this he would have exposed the fraud. However, realistically speaking, if he were to encounter the situation in an auditor's ordinary examination of transactions, where possibly 99.99% of all transactions are bona fide, the question is, "Would he really pursue verification of the installation of the new electric line?" It is not likely.

Obviously, if an auditor checked everything out this thoroughly he or she would not get much done, and would probably still not find any fraud. The proactive fraud auditor can only use his or her judgment in performing a variety of procedures in the hope of getting lucky. Regardless of the auditor's findings, however, his or her examination and line of questioning will not go unnoticed by the undiscovered perpetrator. Very likely, the auditor will be regarded as a risk by that perpetrator, producing a deterrent effect on future frauds.

A previous case described a broker who participated in a shell fraud with office supply store managers. Ball-point pens were ordered and paid for but never delivered. These were shell payment frauds. As with many frauds, discovery frequently depends on the auditor's making a satisfactory determination that the goods or services were in fact delivered.

8. *Defective Delivery.* This is a variation of defective pricing fraud. Simply stated, it usually involves—through a wide variety of means—(1) shipping more merchandise than was legitimately sold, or (2) receiving less merchandise than was purchased and paid for.

For example, assume that 5000 widgets were purchased, and have just been delivered to Company A's warehouse receiving dock by a commercial freight carrier. The person checking the goods at the receiving dock checks the delivery and signs for the receipt of 5000 widgets. The problem is that the carrier had dropped off 200 of the widgets before he arrived at Company A, and only 4800 were delivered. The freight carrier and the Company A receiving foreman are in collusion to steal widgets.

Company A's perpetual inventory records are updated to reflect that 5000 widgets were received. The shortage is not discovered until a physical inventory count is made. When disclosed, attention is frequently focused on the question, "How did the merchandise get out of the warehouse?" When, in fact, it never got in.

Defective shipping fraud works much the same way. Depending on the internal control system in effect, Company A's sales department could feasibly initiate the necessary paperwork to cause a shipment of merchandise to be shipped to Customer X, a confederate. Pains would be taken to assure that the paperwork that should go to the accounting department does not arrive there. The warehouse and the shipping dock would process the shipment, based on the paperwork, but no record of the shipment would ever be entered as a sale, an inventory reduction, or an account receivable. The merchandise would simply be gone.

Evidence of a bold scheme of this sort occurred a number of years ago. It was reported that certain persons would visit building construction sites in the Chicago area and make it known that they would deliver any tools available in the Montgomery Ward catalog at half price. An interested buyer needed only give the M W catalog number, and a week or so later the tool would be delivered. We are not aware of "how" this defective delivery scheme worked. But, since the merchandise being sold was selectively and expeditiously being removed from M W warehouses, it seems more than likely that it was clearing their internal security.

In an instance involving the government, an alert auditor happened to be shopping in a surplus store in New Jersey one day and noticed an item of office furniture—a telephone desk—in a box that still bore a government stock number. He copied the number and the next day checked it out. To his surprise he found that it was an item of new design that had recently been delivered to government warehouse stocks, but which had not yet been sold to government customers. Investigation disclosed that a commercial freight carrier and a government warehouse employee had conspired to deliver less than the quantity purchased. The warehouse employee had falsely certified that the full quantity had been received.

As in the earlier example, detection of missing widgets is often difficult. Since the available records indicate that 5000 were received, there is a natural tendency to look to warehouse and shipping security to explain the inventory shortages. Anytime inventory shortages are experienced and explanations are not readily evident, we recommend that a careful examination of receiving, inventory stock control, and shipping control systems be accomplished. In fact, these examinations should be performed periodically without the "incentives" of unexplained shortages. As with all internal controls, the periodic examinations should include (1) an evaluation of processing system designs and (2) a determination that the systems as designed and approved are being followed.

In the illustration of the missing widgets, it is likely that a fraud auditor performing a competent review of the inventory control system would have found flaws in the receiving document processing system, which allowed the fraud to occur. For example, it is obvious that the warehouse receiving the widgets either was not counting the stock received or did not communicate its count to accounting's inventory control.

In addition to fraud involving disparities in the quantities of items shipped or received, it may also involve the quality of a service or product received. For example, a victim may have ordered and paid for the 'best' quality of some product, and had a lower quality substituted. That is, brand "x" is substituted for brand "y". In another not uncommon fraud, the victim may have ordered and paid for *two* coats of paint to be applied, and received only one coat! One victim of such a fraud eventually began requiring painting contractors to include a slightly different tint to the first coat so that a scratch test could be used to determine that two coats had indeed been applied.

FRAUD AUDITING TECHNIQUE

The task of discovering fraud is so difficult that the fraud auditor often finds that comprehensively examining transactions for fraud requires an inordinate amount of time and does not allow coverage of more than a few transactions in a reasonable time frame. *We do not always recommend comprehensive reviews of transactions to eliminate all or most possibilities of fraud.* As mentioned earlier, we frequently advise fraud auditors to decide what type of fraud they choose to examine a transaction for. They should then limit their examination to a review of whatever evidence is needed to clear the transaction in the event that indicia of fraud is not found, even though some other type of fraud could be present. We have labeled this fraud auditing technique *end auditing*. In other words, if an auditor decides to look for defective deliveries of building maintenance items, for example, we recommend that he or she not waste time examining purchase orders, receiving reports (which can easily be forged or involve collusion), canceled checks, and the like. Rather, we recommend that they go directly to the site of the work and inspect it as may be necessary to determine that it has in fact been fully delivered. By the simple procedure of end auditing the fraud auditor can maximize his or her coverage of many transactions in a given time frame.

In testing a transaction or event, the fraud auditor tends to think in terms of what fraud could occur, and then makes audit tests to determine if it has occurred. If it has not occurred, the test is over. The fraud auditor, selecting the payment of $25,000 for replacing a roof, for example, is likely to first look at the roof to determine that it was in fact replaced. It may not have been, in which case the auditor would immediately institute special fraud search procedures.

If the roof was replaced, the auditor might then decide to extend her review to determine if a double payment fraud is involved. She would then attempt to seek evidence as to when the roof was replaced and by whom. If no suspicious findings are discovered, she could rightly pass the transaction and go on to her next selection, although she would be free at any time to extend her review, depending upon her sense of what might be appropriate.

In a roof replacement, for example, the experienced fraud auditor is always aware that any of the following fraud scenarios can be present:

- The building manager could be in a conspiracy with the roofing contractor, and the work may never have been done. Or the work may have been done by another contractor, but also billed by the building manager's conspiring associate.
- The $25,000 could be a duplicate payment passed through two or three months after the work was done.
- A cheaper roof than contracted for might have been installed.
- In soliciting contractor bids the dimensions of the roof may have been overstated.

In end auditing, the auditor is continually thinking the question, What if . . . ? and then working backward from the assumption. In doing so, he or she is thinking like a perpetrator about all the different ways that fraud could occur in any given transaction. To accomplish end auditing successfully, the auditor must be knowledgeable about the many schemes that a perpetrator could possibly use to defraud.

Incidentally, end auditing is particularly useful in attempting to discover off-the-books fraud, since there is no discrete paper trail or audit trail to follow.

Where to Get Fraud Auditing Experience

Generally speaking, there are today very few auditors who can truly say that they are experienced in fraud auditing. This is because most auditors have few opportunities to audit actual fraud and to learn from experience. When they do confront fraud on the job, it is often the case that they do not recognize the fraud soon enough or at all, and are likely to only learn in retrospect, that is, from their mistakes. Unfortunately, that is the most difficult way to learn—and survive. And there is no university, to our knowledge which teaches the art of fraud auditing.

Initially, there is only one way to get useful fraud experience, and that is from people who have had experience with fraud, such as authors and instructors who are experienced in fraud discovery and control. These are people whose brains you can pick and learn from, people who can take you through cases of actual fraud, teach you tricks, expose you to a wide variety of cases to improve your fraud recognition skills; people who can exercise your mind in fraud recognition and generally save you and your employer from learning about fraud the hard way. Once you have received your initial training you will at a minimum be aware of the fact that fraud exists, and you will be armed with some of the fundamental tools needed to commence your fraud auditing career. From then on it is critical that you maintain a data base of experiences, both successful experiences and failures. You will develop the practices that work best for you.

FRAUD AUDITING

Within your organization you may be the only trained fraud auditor, or you may be one of many. The number of individuals and the financial and other support resources available in your company will depend primarily on the attitude of your top managers toward fraud auditing. As a practical matter, if you are the only one in your company engaged in fraud auditing, your efforts may be on a part-time basis. You may rotate from fraud auditing assignments to more traditional management accounting or internal auditing efforts. In some instances this may be a desirable way to expand your fraud auditing education and skills. The time away from fraud auditing may give you the opportunity to ponder some of the things you did that were useful and some of the things that you might have done. As you develop, your data base of successes and failures will increase.

If you are one of many individuals in your company who have initial training in fraud auditing, you will have the added benefit of learning from the successes and failures of your peers. Additionally, it may be desirable for you to rotate into other traditional management accounting and internal auditing assignments. This serves two useful purposes. Rotation permits you the time needed to ponder your recent experiences and to develop new ideas for future testing and possible implementation in your practice of fraud auditing. Rotation also increases the number of individuals within the company who have fraud auditing experience.

With the current increasing rate of fraud disclosures, many of which are accidental, there is a growing interest in fraud in the audit community. With the demand for fraud training, more and more fraud training experiences are becoming available. Some of them are very good, but some provide little training per se. Avoid courses that are taught by persons without "hands on" experience, who obtain their experience secondhand from research of those fraud cases that are in the public domain. Keep in mind that very few fraud cases are prosecuted and, hence, made public. Many of the toughest cases are not prosecuted, often because the auditors and investigators are unable to gather sufficient evidence to prosecute. Your opportunities to learn from their frustrations in not having the evidence needed to prosecute, and the lessons they learned in the process, are invaluable.

8

CASE STUDIES AND SUGGESTED SOLUTIONS

In planning the content of the *Management Accountants' Guide to Fraud Discovery and Control*, we were at first undecided (1) whether to include case studies involving fraud and, if they were to be included, (2) in what format they would be presented. It was decided not to include actual case studies typically included in publications on the subject of fraud because

- They tend to be included more for interest value than for instruction. It is the serious intention of the authors to provide the reader with lessons that he or she can remember and apply.
- They tend to be too inflexible, complicated, and involved for efficient lesson delivery and comprehension, if the actual facts are restated.
- They tend to lack unpublished details since only facts necessary for prosecution are made public. This detracts from their lesson value.
- Actual examples of some frauds that we wanted to demonstrate are not in the public domain at all.

However, we felt it important to include a number of case studies, essentially for these reasons:

- Case studies impart a reality to the text material.

- Case studies provide practical illustrations of the mechanics of fraud, and of the many variations in which fraud can manifest itself.

- Case studies offer an excellent teaching opportunity to provide audit comments specifically on a given set of case circumstances.

- We believe that there is value in auditors being exposed to various examples of fraud cases because they tend to become "templates" of a sort in the reader's mind. Once they are established, should the reader at some future date encounter facts and circumstances that conform to one or more of his or her mental templates, it is more likely that fraud recognition will occur.

It was decided to include case studies that are based on actual happenings, some of which were prosecuted and some of which were not. Some of the case studies are composed of elements from two or more cases so as to serve the multiple purposes intended. All names are ficticious, and circumstances have been disguised to preclude association with actual events.

In the cases that follow, we suggest that the reader ponder the circumstances presented in each case and consider the fraud possibilities. Usually, more than a single answer is desired. The reader should attempt to test his or her skills by jotting down the fraud possibilities before checking the possible solutions that we suggest. Remember, there are no incorrect answers. If you can conceive of an opportunity to commit fraud, given the bare circumstances we present, it is worth considering by the fraud auditor or investigator. Only logical fraud possibilities are to be considered, the determination of which is roughly the process that a fraud auditor or investigator must go through before beginning his or her search for evidence.

CASE 1. THE WATER TANK

The Situation

You are the auditor for the Bluebird Corporation. The Bluebird plant, located in La Crosse, Wisconsin, comprises many buildings which house general and administrative services, manufacturing operations, and shipping, receiving, and warehousing functions.

Bluebird's management has recently become sensitized to the corporations vulnerability to fraud, after hearing of experiences elsewhere, and you are instructed to devote some of your time to searching for evidence of it.

One day, in compliance with management's request, you make a random selection of payment transactions. The first one you select for examination is a $5000 payment that was made to the Aztec Company. You retrieve the purchase order that required the work that was done and find that it called for the following:

1. Drain 5000 gallon water tank atop Building 12.
2. Scrape and clean interior surfaces of tank.
3. Rehabilitate surfaces as may be necessary.
4. Coat all interior surfaces of tank with Z-26 Sealant, an elastomeric waterproofing and rustproofing compound.
5. Refill tank with 5000 gallons of water.
6. Perform and complete all work during plant vacation shutdown period August 1–14, 1990.

What Is Required

Play the role of the Bluebird Corporation auditor at this point. Jot down on a piece of paper *specifically* all types of fraud that are possible in this transaction, and what you plan to do to check out each one of them.

Be explicit in detailing the frauds that are possible. For example, one of the frauds present could be a duplicate payment. Expand on this observation by writing a short scenario such as, "Paula Jones, a Bluebird Corporation accounting clerk, acting in collusion with John Swanson, an accountant from the Aztec Company, caused the submission of a duplicate invoice to be submitted and paid. Swanson, the Aztec employee, cooperated by noting that the invoice had been paid twice and caused a refund check to be issued to the attention of Paula Jones, his coconspirator at Bluebird."

Note: If you are going to be successful at discovering fraud, you must get in the habit of focusing on people who have the *opportunity* to commit fraud, even though there is no reason to believe that they have done so. Some auditors have a problem with using this technique in the early stages of fraud auditing, claiming that people are innocent until proven guilty, and that they shouldn't be examined as though they were guilty without good cause. Accordingly, they prefer *not* to investigate the Paula Joneses of this world, who in the vast majority of instances are innocent of any crime. This latter attitude is very commendable, but it will not catch the Paula Joneses who *are* guilty of fraud.

Focusing upon the Paula Joneses who have opportunity will give you many chances to discover evidence of fraud. Remember, it is extremely unlikely that Paula will commit fraud only once. Accordingly, if you examine many of the things that Paula has done, if she is a perpetrator, your chances of finding evidence are excellent. However, always remember that you must be particularly careful to secure your work papers and not to make it obvious that you are focusing on her. In the end, you may have found no reason to further suspect Paula. The lack of evidence will have proven her innocence.

For Your Guidance

For the purposes of this case study only, ignore your time restraints. That is, in a real life situation it would be wholly impractical for you to check out every possibility of fraud for a transaction that was selected at random and for which you had no reason to believe that fraud might be present. For practical reasons, in a real-life situation your checking would have to be selective.

In addition, be practical in suggesting what you would do to check out fraud possibilities.

Suggested Solution

The "water tank" case was selected for the leading presentation because it offers a wide variety of possible fraudulent actions and because our water tank could be just about any project occurring in your particular business or agency environment.

In pondering the water tank case, if you jotted down a scenario for just about every sort of fraud we mentioned in Chapter 7, you were correct. For example:

CASE 1. THE WATER TANK

1. About the simplest fraud that might have occurred is a duplicate payment. That is, the $5000 payment for rehabilitating the water tank could have been paid twice to the Aztec Company. Collusion is usually not necessary for the fraud to work; that is, Mary Jones, an accounting clerk at Bluebird could simply process a duplicate copy of the Aztec invoice for payment—forging any necessary signatures—and hope to intercept either the check when it was returned by Aztec, or the Aztec refund of the $5000. However, a company like Bluebird usually has a measure of internal control present which would preclude Mary's receiving incoming cash receipts.

Accordingly, the fraud would work more reliably if Mary acted in collusion with her boyfriend, Tom Jones, who works for Aztec. When the Bluebird duplicate check for $5000 is received at Aztec, it would be deposited. Then, Tom would see to it that Aztec writes a refund check for $5000 to Bluebird, and would either assure that Mary receives the check, or cash it himself, splitting the receipts with Mary.

An attempt at audit discovery would most likely include a review of all payments to Aztec—probably a computer scan—for identical payment amounts.

At this point you should begin thinking as a fraud perpetrator would think. That is, "If an auditor could detect the duplicate payment by scanning for identical amounts, and if I have a conspirator at the Aztec Company, why not have an invoice prepared in a dissimilar amount?" Read on.

2. If you thought a double payment fraud might be possible, you would be correct. In other words, the perpetrator could arrange for an identical invoice to be submitted from the "Larson Company." The double payment fraud would be just a bit more difficult for the perpetrator to carry off; however, it offers him or her a little more protection in that it is slightly more difficult for the auditor to discover. All supporting documentation that the auditor might choose to review would appear to authenticate the job. It would be properly authorized, and receipt would be confirmed. There is an invoice from the Larson Company, and a canceled check. Where do you go from there?

The auditor's discovery that the job was done by Aztec, and not Larson, would be a little more difficult. A purchase order can easily be forged. The job was done properly—why would the auditor have cause to suspect that the Larson Company did not do the work?—

unless by sheer chance he or she also happened to select the Aztec invoice, an extremely unlikely occurrence in a large company. One caution here: do not be naive and say how easy it would be to determine that Aztec did the work and not Larson. Remember, at this point you have no reason to suspect that this occurred.

Detecting the double payment fraud is a bit more difficult than the duplicate payment fraud. Scanning payments to Larson gives you no clues. Detection would have to begin with your decision to check for double payment fraud, even though you have no reason to do so. You would then proceed to special procedures designed to determine if Larson actually did the work. We will leave that process to your imagination. Another possibility for determining the double payment fraud depends on other measurement systems (internal controls) that may be operative in the business or agency involved. For example, the company may maintain a maintenance record on the water tank. If so, check it out to determine any clues that might indicate suspiciously repetitive maintenance projects.

The double payment fraud almost always involves conspiracy, especially where the "Larson Company" is an existing contractor, and not a fiction.

3. If you thought a kickback might be involved, you would again be correct. It is quite possible that the work may have been worth only $4000 and that Della Ware, the Bluebird purchasing agent, steered the business to Aztec in return for a kickback of a portion of the $1000 excess.

To detect the possibility of a kickback, again, you would first have to presume that it was a possibility and then seek pricing information that would prove or disprove your supposition. In reviewing the acquisition of products or services of any kind the fraud auditor must have a sense of what the product or service should cost. If he or she does not, there will be little chance of ever detecting kickbacks, which are without question among the most common of frauds. Kickbacks of any significant amounts are always recovered by the provider in the prices charged for the products or services being sold.

Kickbacks are very difficult to detect, but with persistence you can get lucky. The auditor must establish points of reference for what

CASE 1. THE WATER TANK

things should cost. Often it is necessary to refer to past prices paid, catalogs, offers from other suppliers, and so forth. One illustration involves an auditor who happened to be reviewing unit prices charged to the government on an open contract for portable dictating machines. For the sizable quantities being purchased by government agencies, he became curious as to why the contract unit price was $300 each. During his lunch hour he walked down the street to a small office supply store and inquired about the price of an identical item. The proprietor offered to sell it to him for $225.

Of course, there are no catalogs or ready references that indicate what refurbishing a water tank would cost. However, perhaps it was company policy for the purchasing agent to solicit bids from various contractors. If so, an abstract should be available for your inspection. Perhaps formal bid offers were required. If so, review them.

Assuming that the auditor finds a price disparity between the purchase order price and the competitive price, she is far from being finished with her fraud case. In fact, in most instances, auditors will "blow" their possible fraud cases at this point by reporting the price discrepancies, with a gleeful "look what I found" attitude. Since one example of this sort *does not make a fraud case*, a possible actual perpetrator of fraud will very likely be seen only as having made a minor pricing "mistake."

The experienced fraud auditor, however, will not report her finding of the pricing error. Instead, she will subsequently proceed to examine other purchasing agreements that her suspect entered into. If she finds more, she is on her way to making her fraud case. The presumption here is that a competent purchasing agent does not repeatedly make that sort of error. At this point, the assistance of a competent criminal investigator should be retained to determine if a prosecutable case is possible.

4. If you thought a defective delivery fraud might be involved, you could be correct. Before reading further, however, stop and think for a moment about how the delivery of the water tank job could be defective.

Having thought about it for a few minutes, you recall that the purchase order for the job required that the tank interior be coated with Z-26, an expensive waterproofing substance. What if the tank

113

were not coated at all? Or what if the tank were coated with a cheaper product? Since Bluebird is paying for the expensive Z-26 coating, the application of anything less would very likely constitute fraud.

Once again we will leave it to your creative imagination as to how to determine whether Z-26 was applied. Would you check the receiving report to see if the application of Z-26 was noted? Or you could perhaps check with the responsible Bluebird Corporation building manager? Read on for a better solution.

5. If you thought a shell payment might be involved, you were correct. In fact, the actual case from which this one was taken involved a shell payment.

The actual auditors involved in the water tank case at that time were experiencing many defective deliveries and, as a result, were taking extraordinary measures to determine that their employer was getting what he bargained for. Having selected the water tank payment transaction at random, they retained the services of an experienced building maintenance technician and went directly to the building involved, where they contacted the building manager. He verified that the water tank had been cleaned to the purchase order specifications. The auditor replied that they were going to check it out anyway. The building manager laughed at them saying, "How will you do that? It's full of water and high in the air." At that point, the technician that accompanied the auditors went to the top of the building, climbed a ladder to the top of the water tank, and slid back the access cover at the top of the tank. He then rolled up his sleeve and reached as deep into the tank as he could, dragging his fingers up the side. When he withdrew his arm he had a handful of rust and scale. The tank had never been refurbished. The receiving reports had been falsified by the building manager.

Of course, had he not come up with the rust and scale, the next step would have been to take a sample of the coating material for analysis to determine that it was in fact Z-26.

Sounds like a lot to expect of fraud auditors? It is. Is there any question as to why traditional auditing does not detect this sort of fraud? There shouldn't be. As a matter of fact, fraud auditors should not be expected to detect all frauds either. The possibilities are just too numerous. However, by adhering to general standards and field standards for fraud auditing, they have a much better chance of detecting fraud, and in so doing, they raise the risk for the perpetrator.

CASE 2.   THE PARKING LOT

The Situation

The second transaction, #89-6344, that you have selected for examination is a September 30, 1989, payment for $250,000 made to the First Class Paving Company. You look up the Bluebird work order that initiates the procurement action and find that it calls for:

Advertised procurement: "Resurface Employee Parking Lot #2 with 4" layer of bituminous concrete, and seal surface with Formula X. No repairs to existing lot surface are necessary." Signed: Plant Superintendent, Sam Diego.

In the file you also find the Request for Proposals (RFP) that was sent out to six interested contractors. It is exactly the same as the work order above, except that it provides this additional information: "Parking lot is 250,000 square feet ($500' \times 500'$)". The RFP is signed by the Bluebird grounds manager, Sam Francisco.

What Is Required

Again, play the role of the Bluebird Corporation auditor. Jot down on a piece of paper *specifically* all types of fraud that are possible in this transaction and what you plan to do to check out each one of them.

Be explicit in detailing *all* the frauds that you can think of. For example, one of the frauds present could be a double payment. Expand on this observation by writing a short scenario about how it could happen. Assign any fictitious personal and company names you wish to clarify the mechanics of each fraud type. (There are more than two frauds possible.)

From the listing of fraud types that you have prepared, select two of them for actual testing. Remember, in fraud auditing, the transactions that you select at random for examination will be largely legitimate. You are literally looking for a needle in a haystack, and you cannot afford to spend unlimited time checking out all possibilities for every one. Accordingly, to obtain some coverage over a maximum number of transactions in a limited time, we recommend only selective examination of each transaction. With experience, fraud auditors tend to develop a sense as to which aspects of a given transaction, in a given environment, should be reviewed more thoroughly. Nevertheless, for this case, "The Parking Lot," select two fraud possibilities and describe what further testing you would recommend and why. What would you look for? Be explicit. Specifically state whom you would contact, what information you would ask for, and so on. Be thorough but practical.

For Your Guidance

Be creative!

Suggested Solution

The parking lot fraud case is taken from an actual event. However, like the water tank case, it conceivably could involve almost the entire gamut of garden variety frauds. If you have guessed the type of fraud that actually occurred, you may go to the head of the class.

By now there should be no doubt in your mind that it is possible to have a duplicate payment fraud, a double payment fraud, or a shell payment fraud on just about any transaction. Accordingly, we will not discuss these possibilities further, although in actual fraud auditing practice you must never ignore them as possibilities.

Note that the parking lot case was an "advertised" contract. There is a general consensus that advertised contracts protect entities from a variety of frauds. Many businesses, governmental agencies, universities, and the like believe that advertising the award of a contract assures the entity of the best price and protects it from fraud. They believe that the advertisement process allows all interested suppliers to provide a bid, and as a result assures that the lowest price protects their interests. Those who believe that are wrong. As a matter of fact, use of the advertised acquisition process is often one of the worst ways to let a contract. Assuming that everyone is honest, of course, it is a good process. However, not everyone is honest.

A contract such as that for the parking lot, for example, could have been reopened after the award was made (although it was not) for some "essential" reason. For example, in advertising the contract it could have been determined that the company neglected to specify that it wanted lanes painted. Or perhaps, on the more expensive side, the company could have determined that the lot needed more than a mere resurfacing. Perhaps some excavation was decided upon, and perhaps drainage work needed to be done. These post-award changes often are the basis for fraud.

The way it works is that an influential conspirator within the company informs his contractor conspirator to bid low to be sure to get the contract award. This is also known as "steering" the award. The bid may be so low as to give the bidder no profit, or even to result in a loss were he required to deliver on the contract as it was written. If the parking lot contract were rigged in this manner, the subsequent requirement for the contractor to excavate portions of the lot, install drainage pipes, and paint necessary stripes would have cost Bluebird dearly. Of course, in cases where the reopened contract device is used to defraud a victim, the contract is rarely so simple as that for our parking lot. However, the process is virtually the same for large contracts.

We have seen this device used primarily in the construction of buildings. Often, when a building is to be constructed, especially if it is a large building, there are literally thousands of ways to change the building specifications to allow large profits to be built into the cost of making the changes. Many are "preplanned," of course. Sometimes it will be noticed that the building is oriented to the north when it should be to the south. The charge can be very expensive. Of course, the conspiring contractor will always claim that construction was under way when the change was made and that this occasioned considerable scrap and lost costs. However, a conspiring contractor will be able to anticipate the changes and will in actuality minimize his scrap and lost costs, but not disclose that fact in his claim.

In the case of the parking lot, you should have jotted down that there was a possibility for a defective delivery. Even though the Bluebird grounds manager, Sam Francisco, signed the receiving report certifying that the lot was in fact delivered as 2 inches thick, and was in fact sealed with Formula X, we now know that people like Sam sometimes have reason to lie. Or perhaps he was just lazy and did not check the lot at all. If you chose to visit the site of the work—which we always recommend in fraud auditing—you would have determined that the lot was not a shell payment, and you would have the opportunity to determine that the 2-inch thickness was provided and that Formula X was applied. You may not have been competent to do that personally, but you could have brought along someone who was. In this case, let us further assume that your tests turned out negative.

Give some thought to what actually happened in the real case this was taken from. Defective pricing is involved. Before reading further, try to figure out how.

Frequently, contractors responding to simple requests for proposals of this type, which are very specific as to the work to be done, will provide their bids without visting the site. In fact, it is often inconvenient to visit the site if area security is maintained. Entry passes must be obtained, and of course in the case of our parking lot, it will usually be overflowing with employee cars. Preparing a bid is often a simple matter of multiplying the square footage of the lot by the contractor's price per square foot. In this case, First Class Paving bid $1 a square foot × 250,000 to get its bid of $250,000. For your information, the other contractors submitting bids offered prices per square foot ranging from $1.10 to $1.30.

By now you should have figured out what the fraud was. The parking lot was actually only 450' × 450'! Did you think to measure the lot? If you did you may stay at the head of the class. By the way, who do you think the inside conspirator may be?

CASE 3. THE STORAGE BUILDINGS

The Situation

The Upson Corporation decides to build three new identical storage buildings to ease the overloading of its existing warehouses and to meet the need for additional storage in the next few years if its sales continue to grow as expected. Management authorizes the Contract Division to proceed with construction plans. The entire project is expected to cost about $1,200,000.

A Request for Bids is prepared and mailed to all interested contractors, together with building specifications and other necessary particulars. Contractors are also instructed that the buildings were to be built sequentially and that progress payments will be allowed at the 50% completion point for each building and at completion of each building (less a 10% holdback at each stage).

At the bid opening six weeks later, four bidders submit proposals to construct the buildings, as follows:

The Pence Company	$1,000,000
Builder B	$1,100,000
Builder C	$1,200,000
Builder D	$1,300,000

The Pence Company is selected as the lowest qualified bidder, and is awarded the construction contract.

What Is Required

Speculate on what could possibly be wrong here. If you have insufficient information, what additional information would you like to see?

Suggested Solution

Admittedly, it is extremely unlikely that this case would occur this simply in real life, and it did not, at least to our knowledge. It is easier to appreciate this form of fraud through a simple example. In actuality, it can get quite complicated.

After reading the case situation, did you have any comments or a request for additional information?

Actually, there may be nothing wrong with the contract. However, were you to have asked for the Pence Company's estimated costs of building each of the three buildings you may have noticed a troubling imbalance. These were their costs submitted for each building and made a part of their contract:

Building 1	$600,000
Building 2	$300,000
Building 3	$100,000

These statistics suggest the possibility that an unbalanced contract fraud may be pending. The difficult thing about an unbalanced contract fraud is that at the time the contract is written, although there may be intent to commit fraud, no fraud has been or may be committed. It is difficult for an auditor, at the contracting stage, to even suggest that there is fraudulent intent.

To begin with, it is probably not a sound business practice for the Upson Corporation to agree to the wide variation in unit prices. The first building is priced at nearly twice the average cost of the three buildings. This means that when Upson pays the Pence Company $600,000 (less 10%) upon its completion, should the Pence Company default on the rest of the contract, Upson will have paid $540,000 for a building that is worth considerably less, by any account. However, this is not the fraud that we are going for.

On the other hand, it is not unusual for a contractor faced with a contract of this sort to charge more for the first building, because he logically would have certain start-up costs for building 1 that would not apply to buildings 2 and 3. Earth moving may be required, equipment must be brought to the construction site, and inventories of materials purchased. Hence, an unbalanced contract, per se, is not necessarily of fraudulent intent. This is what makes audit evaluation of this type of fraud difficult.

Given the facts presented, however, and assuming that the unbalancing does *not* represent start-up costs, ask yourself these questions: "What happens if building 3 is canceled?" "What if the cancellation of building 3 was intended before the contract bid solicitation was advertised?" Let us further assume that the increase in business that the Upson Corporation anticipated when the three buildings were authorized, did not materialize, creating a legitimate reason for canceling the third building.

This is the way the unbalanced contract fraud works when it is "intended." There is *always* an inside conspirator and a vendor or contractor who is also in on the conspiracy. They "arrange" certain contract specifications that are dependent upon the inside conspirator's assuring that certain actions will come to pass. Since non-conspiring contracts have no such assurance, they are at an obvious disadvantage. We will try to make this a bit clearer with other case studies. However, consider that it is quite possible that the Pence Company, in submitting a low bid to build the three buildings for

$1,000,000 when the Upson Corporation estimated that they would cost $1,200,000, may not have been able to make a profit had they been required to complete all three buildings.

Assuming further that there *is* fraudulent intent in this case, it would be extremely difficult to make a prosecutable case, even if the second two buildings were canceled. Our recommendation here to aspiring fraud auditors would be to gather as many facts about the present case as possible, without disclosing the fact that you consider the transaction suspicious. At least initially, under no circumstances be critical of the contract. However, as we have stressed earlier in this handbook, be mindful of the fact that "a crook is a crook is a crook." Attempt to determine the name of the person who is the likely inside conspirator and, as secretly as possible, begin to review other projects in which he or she was instrumental. Be alert also to projects that are under way. If the person had fraudulent intent in the storage buildings contract, it is likely that there will be other examples using a similar modus operandi. Find two or more examples in which unbalanced contracts, or other schemes, resulted in excess costs for the Upson Corporation, and you may very well have a prosecutable case of fraud. At the very least, you will have sufficient cause to recommend that the insider's employment be terminated.

One of the next several cases will have a more sophisticated variation of the unbalanced contract fraud scheme. See if you can detect it before reading the solution.

CASE 4.   LESSOR VARIABLE COST "PASS THROUGH"

For Your Information

(The following is provided in recognition of the fact that many readers are likely to be unfamiliar with the variable cost features of many longer-term commercial leases. If you are familiar with commercial leasing practices, you may skip to "The Situation.")

Long-term commercial real estate leases often provide for two-part rental cost formulas, out of an understandable concern on the part of building owners over their inability to predict the uncontrollable future costs of inflation, such as for heat, light, power, taxes, custodial services, and so on.

They are equitable for both building owners and tenants. With such rental agreements, building owners are more likely to enter into long-term leases, protected from unpredictable operating cost fluctuations, and tenants are able to assure long-term occupancy at reasonably predictable and equitable costs of occupancy.

The first part of the two-part rent formula involves the fixed cost of the real estate itself, wherein the property owner basically recovers his investment cost plus profit. It remains the same throughout the term specified in the lease, which is usually throughout the firm term plus option periods. The second part of the rent formula is the computation of all costs other than those included in the first part. They include, basically, the costs of operating the building and are expected to vary (increase?) from year to year as a result of inflation and other factors. The second part of the formula is called a "pass through," so named because it allows the owner to pass on all the variable costs to tenants. The pass-through feature is normally intended to assure that the owner will break even, with neither a loss nor a profit.

The Situation

The Bluebird Corporation leases office and parking space in a relatively new building in Washington, D.C.

The Building Management Corporation (BMC) manages the building for a trust. The building contains 500,000 square feet of rentable office and ground floor commercial space. Enclosed basement parking space is also available for rent to tenants on a priority basis. All building tenant rental costs are determined on the basis of a two-part formula:

1. A fixed cost-per-square-foot base rate, which never changes throughout firm term or option periods, intended to provide for the owner's recovery of "real property" cost and profit.

2. An annual proration, or "pass through," of the annual cost of operating the building, to be allocated to tenants equitably, based on the ratio of the office and commercial space rented by *each* tenant, to the total rentable office and commercial space in the building.

CASE 4. LESSOR VARIABLE COST "PASS THROUGH"

The Bluebird lease with BMC provides for:

A. 40,000 square feet:
25,000 square feet office space @ $25/sq. ft.
15,000 square feet of enclosed basement parking @ $5/sq. ft.
Plus annual pass through:

B. 5 years firm term occupancy.

C. Two 5-year renewal options at the same rates.

In your capacity as a controller for the Bluebird Corporation, you look over the $1,300,000 rental charge for 1990 (year 4 of the firm term). The BMC management firm has provided the following disclosure in support of its 1990 rent invoice:

Building Management Corporation
Bluebird Corporation 1990 Rental Charges

Bluebird Corporation estimated 1990 rental cost:

Base rate rental 40,000 sq. ft.	$ 700,000
Pass-through costs @ $15/sq. ft.	$ 600,000
Total 1990 rent (estimated)	$1,300,000
Monthly payments (1/12)	$ 108,333

Basis for pass-through rate:
Estimated 1990 building operating costs $7,125,000
Net total office and commercial space occupied* 475,000 sq. ft.
$ divided by sq. ft. = $15.00/sq. ft.

*Total office and commercial space 500,000 sq. ft.
Less: 50,000 sq. ft. space to be vacant 6 months (January 1 through June 30).

In the corner of the BMC billing you notice the inked stamp used by the Bluebird Corporation and the initials of John Frankfurt, director of the Bluebird Real Estate Management Division, who has reviewed and approved the estimated 1990 BMC billing.

What Is Required

Review the case and jot down your comments:

1. Note the "propriety" of the Bluebird lease contract.
2. Note any possible indicia of fraud that may be present.
3. If you suspect fraud, describe it, quantify it (approximately), comment on who the "players" might be, and describe what actions you would take.
4. If there are no indicia of fraud evident in the above particulars, what are the possibilities for fraud, if any?

Suggested Solution

The solution to this case study is relatively simple, provided that you know that fraud is present and look for it. Admittedly, it is simple in execution. The most interesting aspect about this particular fraud is that there is good reason to believe that it endured for many years in a very large combination office and commercial building in a major U.S. city. In fact, it may be still going on. We learned about it from a friend, who had discovered it for one of the tenants of the building. We are not aware of any prosecution that resulted.

Solution (1). In 1990 the lessor's pass-through costs were correctly estimated at $7,125,000 as he claimed. However, his formula for allocating the $7,125,000 to tenants was faulty and ended up prorating much more than $7,125,000. He computed his allocation rate, as he should have, on the basis of his office and commercial space. But then he applied the rate to the tenants' gross square footage rented—including parking space. Since Bluebird Corporation occupies 25,000 square feet of office space, and 15,000 square feet of parking space, they were overcharged for pass-through costs by 60% (25,000 = 100%, 15,000 = 60%).

Solution (2). The "readers of fine print" probably noticed that the rental arrangements provide that the pass-through rate should be computed on the basis of the total *rentable* space, and not the total *rented* space. The BMC deduction of 25,000 square feet for the space vacant during January 1 through June 30 is improper. The building owners are personally responsible for the pass-through costs allocable to the vacant space and should not have passed it on the tenants.

CASE 5. THE VENETIAN BLINDS

It is difficult to understand how the lessor could not have had fraudulent intent in practicing what was described in this case study. Certainly, at the close of his fiscal year, were the overcharges somehow accidental, the overrecovery of pass-through costs would have been noticed and adjustments made.

If overcharges such as those described in the case study endure for any appreciable period of time after the close of the rental year, without appropriate adjustments, that fact alone seems to confirm that there was fraudulent intent on the part of the landlord. If the overcharges also occurred in prior rental years, the lessor's fraudulent intent would be rather obvious.

The fact that John Frankfurt, director of Bluebird Real Estate Management Division, initialed the rental computation appears to implicate him. It was his responsibility to notice the overcharge, and if he was not involved, he was certainly grossly negligent.

It is indeed surprising that such an overcharge could endure for long, but frequently the simplest of frauds are the most successful. The auditor who discovers such an overcharge must not rush to report his or her find and seek a refund from the building owner. A refund in the event of error can always be obtained. Rather, the auditor must first review the charges from prior years to determine whether they were also in error. With one overcharge, even though there may have been fraudulent intent, it might be difficult to convince a prosecuting attorney. However, if the auditor could show two or more years of overcharges, the attorney would probably be obliged to investigate the building to determine whether other tenants were also overcharged, and prosecution would be likely.

CASE 5. THE VENETIAN BLINDS

The Situation

It is January 11, 1990, and the Bluebird Corporation auditor is randomly examining payment transactions one day, when she comes to you for assistance. One of the transactions that she has selected for further examination is the payment of $7,056 on July 5, 1989, to the Brite Cleaning Company for cleaning venetian blinds.

You are an accounts payable supervisor in the Bluebird general accounting department. The auditor requests several documents relating to the cleaning contract for her review. Specifically, she asks for (1) the purchase order, (2) the receiving report, (3) the contractor's invoice, and (4) the canceled Bluebird check.

You are aware that the auditor is a fraud specialist, and you are disturbed that she is wasting her time reviewing the accounts payable that you supervise. You are proud of the fact that the accounts payable division is well run. You have personally evaluated all of the accounts payable internal controls designed to prevent fraud and/or duplicate payments, and have found them to be adequate and in use. You are confident that the auditor's review will disclose no improprieties.

You watch as she examines the purchase order for the cleaning job. The order, #39485, was properly authorized by Mr. C. Attle, the building services manager. Dated April 15, 1989, it provided for "cleaning venetian blinds in building 12 of the corporate office complex, in accordance with calendar year 1989 cleaning service general contract agreement."

It provided further details as follows: 150 window blinds, all uniformly sized at 6' × 8'. To be started as soon as possible. To be completed by June 30, 1989.

You notice that the auditor makes a note in her work papers that the block at the bottom of the purchase order, which provides space for acknowledging the satisfactory receipt of the services, had been signed on June 29, 1989, by Sam Bernadino, a supervisory cleaning engineer. You know Sam, and you remember when the cleaning order was let. In fact, it was you who had complained to Sam that the blinds needed cleaning, and you remember how pleased you were when it was expeditiously and satisfactorily accomplished.

You learn that the auditor found Mr. Bernadino in the plant and questioned him about the cleaning job. He remembered acknowledging receipt of the services. He adds that "the Brite people always do a good job."

The invoice is #34986, dated June 30, 1989. It states that 150 venetian blinds were cleaned in accordance with Bluebird Corporation purchase order dated April 15, 1989, #39485. Total square footage of blinds cleaned is 7200, at a price of $1 a square foot, or $7200. A 2% cash discount is allowed if paid in 10 days.

CASE 5. THE VENETIAN BLINDS

The Brite Company invoice bears a Bluebird Corporation stamped imprint, which includes the date that the invoice was received and a space that requires a Bluebird designate to approve the invoice for payment. The approval space bears Mr. C. Attle's signature.

The invoice stamp also bears *your* initials approving the payment. The auditor asks you to explain the significance of your initials. You tell her that it is required by the internal controls. That is, before an invoice can be approved for payment, it is your responsibility to assure that it meets the following criteria:

1. There is a valid purchase order signed by a person authorized to order goods or services, and that the amount was within his or her purchasing authority. In the present case, Sam Bernadino is authorized to order building maintenance supplies and services up to $25,000 on his signature alone.

2. There is appropriate evidence that the goods or services were actually received. In this case, Mr. C. Attle, the building 12 manager, had signed the purchase order receiving block. There is no question that the signature was Mr. Attle's, which is unique.

3. There is a bona fide invoice that claims payment for the supplies or services. The manager, or designate, responsible for the expenditure must sign the invoice indicating that all requirements for payment have been complied with. In this case the invoice was signed by Mr. Attle.

You explain that if all of the above conditions are met, you initial the invoice and indicate on it whether or not the prompt payment discount can be taken. You point out that a 2% discount was taken for paying the Brite invoice promptly.

You accompany the auditor when she tours building 12 on August 20. She observes that the blinds are very attractive and that they have obviously been cleaned recently. They look very nice. She visits with some of the employees there, who are pleased with the cleaning job, commenting, "You should have seen the blinds before the Brite Cleaning people started."

127

The auditor is satisfied that the $7,056 payment is proper, takes no exceptions to it, and goes on to the next selection.

What Is Required

1. Was it necessary for the auditor to check the things that she did? What was the purpose of her checks?
2. Did the auditor do enough work? or perhaps too much?
3. Suggest two *possible* fraudulent actions that would not have been disclosed by the steps taken by the auditor, but which could have been proven by available documentation. Be specific.

Suggested Solution

All of the auditor's steps were proper. Whether or not they were all necessary is the auditor's judgment, and we do not choose to second guess her. There were additional steps that she could have taken to check for other types of fraud with regard to the venetian blinds, but to do so would have taken time that she may have wished to devote to other transactions. It should be noted, as was mentioned previously, that in auditing for the presence of fraud, the auditor need not perform a thorough review of a given transaction to eliminate all possibilities of fraud. Were she to do so the review of the venetian blind cleaning could very well take time away from extending her review to other transactions and produce no results, whereas the other transactions may have produced a finding of fraud.

When she personally contacted Mr. Bernadino, she was obviously checking to make sure that it was he who acknowledged receipt of the cleaning. Accordingly, she was assured of satisfactory delivery of the service; that is, providing that Bernadino was not a conspirator to fraud. She must have had some doubts, because she chose to actually visit the scene of the cleaning and personally witnessed that the job was done. Note that she spoke with people in the area and determined (1) that the blinds had needed to be cleaned, and (2) that the Brite people did the work.

There were at least three possible frauds that she did not check out. It is quite possible that (1) a duplicate payment was involved, (2) a double payment was involved, and (3) there was defective pricing of the invoice she examined.

CASE 5. THE VENETIAN BLINDS

Items 1 and 2 above are simple frauds that you can envision without further explanation here. However, the actual case that this example was taken from did, in fact, involve defective pricing. What the auditor failed to do was to examine the 1989 general requirements contract that existed between the Bluebird Corporation and the Brite Company. It was an agreement that provided that Brite would respond to Bluebird's requests for cleaning services during 1989, and *stated the prices that would be charged.* Had she read it, she would have found that the agreement provided that Bluebird would be charged Brite's prevailing rates for cleaning services, "less a discount of 40%." Accordingly, Bluebird was overcharged 40% of the $7200 charge, or $2800.

Had the auditor made this discovery, she would probably have arrived at the following preliminary conclusions and the additional audit program:

1. There is a strong possibility of fraud. The date of the auditor's examination is January 11 1990; the Brite Company has not returned the "overpayment"; and internal management has not officially discovered it.

2. If there is fraud, it is likely that Mr. C. Attle is a conspirator with someone at the Brite Company. It was he who approved the invoice charges as correct. He should have known about the discount. Of course, it could have been negligence on his part. Was he similarly negligent on other suspicious occasions?

3. Additional evidence is needed to conclude on the foregoing. Everything about the 1989 contract should be examined closely. If it was openly advertised, review the advertisement and the returned bids that were received to determine whether it appears that the contract was "steered" to Brite. Does the discount given appear to be competitive?

4. Since the Brite invoice is probably for only one of a number of services performed under the open-end contract for 1989, review all other invoices for services performed under the contract, especially those that involved Mr. C. Attle.

5. Review work done by the Brite people for prior years.

6. Do nothing about reporting the overcharge until the foregoing steps have been satisfactorily resolved.

CASE 6. THE PAINTING TERM CONTRACT

The Situation

The Ten-Twenty Corporation plant had grown explosively in the 1970s and now sprawled over a 200-acre site in suburban St. Louis. Among other things, maintenance of its many aging buildings was a growing problem. Della Ware was the director of plant maintenance. She supervised a small group of Ten-Twenty employees who were usually on call for emergency maintenance services. However, it was customary for her to call on outside contractors to perform most nonemergency plant maintenance work.

Most of the plant maintenance contractors working for the Ten-Twenty Corporation performed more or less continuously at Ten-Twenty, under what are known as "term" contracts. Term contracts are written to provide for specified services, for a specified cost, for a specified term—usually one year. They are used by corporations such as Ten-Twenty so as to have prequalified contractors on call to provide services when needed at previously established unit costs. Term contracts are a way of avoiding the delay and administrative effort of seeking new contractors and negotiating prices each time a service is needed.

Normally, as in the Ten-Twenty term contracts, no quantitative performance requirements are stipulated in term contracts. Contractors merely agree to perform specified services at an agreed-upon reimbursement rate, in return for assurance by the entity involved that they be the sole contractor used for the specified service. Usually, as in the customary Ten-Twenty term contracts, the contractor is assured that he will receive a minimum level of business, for example, $1,000,000, from the entity during the contract period. Term contracts are often let as the result of advertised bids.

One of the maintenance term contracts used by Della Ware was for interior painting. The need for the painting contract arose when a new Ten-Twenty CEO, depressed by the shade of the aging blue paint that covered most corporate office walls, suggested one day in October 1988 that they be repainted—any color, just as long as it was an off-white. Soon after, Della initiated the search for a term-contract painter.

Ten-Twenty Corporation's intention to enter into a term contract for interior painting was advertised in principal trade publications

CASE 6.   THE PAINTING TERM CONTRACT

in the St. Louis area, and interested contractors were instructed to contact the Ten-Twenty Corporation purchasing agent, Jerry Whyte.

All qualified contractors expressing an interest, were provided with the following relevant details and instructions:

Ten-Twenty Corporation Request for Proposal (RFP)

I. All interested painting contractors are invited to submit a proposal to perform under an interior painting term contract for the period of: Calendar Year 1989. The contract will require the contractor to respond to all requests for interior painting made by the Ten-Twenty Corporation Maintenance Division during CY 1989.

II. Proposals should include the proposer's price offer for *each* of the painting requirement categories indicated below.

- The low bidder will be selected on the basis of the lowest aggregate bid.
- The contract will *guarantee* that the performing contractor will receive gross revenues at least equal to his total minimum bid during the contract term.
- The Ten-Twenty Corporation may at its option increase any of the painting requirements, without limitation, at the unit prices offered and accepted.
- The contract will provide for *no* minimum or maximum painting requirement.

Requirements for Submitting Price Proposals

Category A Painting:
Walls order nine (9) feet high, one coat.
Price per square foot × 1,200,000 square feet $_____

Category B Painting:
Walls under nine (9) feet high, two coats.
Price per square foot × 200,000 square feet $_____

Category C Painting:
Walls over nine (9) feet high, one coat.
Price per square foot × 100,00 square feet $_____

Category D Painting:
Walls over nine (9) feet high, two coats.
Price per square foot × 12,500 square feet $_____

Category E Painting:
Ceilings one coat.
Price per square foot × 250,000 square feet $_____

Category F Painting:
Ceilings, two coats.
Price per square foot × 4,000 square feet $_____

Four painting contractors submitted proposals. The following are abstracts of their proposals:

Juliet Company	Category A $.08/square foot × 1,200,000 square feet	$ 96,000
	Category B $.14/square feet × 200,000 square feet	28,000
	Category C $.10/square foot × 100,000 square feet	10,000
	Category D $.16/square foot × 12,500 square feet	2,000
	Category E $.12/square foot × 250,000 square feet	30,000
	Category F $.18/square foot × 4,000 square feet	720
Juliet Company aggregate bid		$166,720
Kilo Company	Category A $.085/square foot × 1,200,000 square feet	$102,000
	Category B $.15/square foot × 200,000 square feet	30,000
	Category C $.095/square foot × 100,000 square feet	9,500
	Category D $.14/square foot × 12,500 square feet	1,750
	Category E $.11/square foot × 250,000 square feet	27,500

Category F $.185/square foot		
× 4,000 square feet		740
Kilo Company aggregate bid		$171,490

Lima Company

Category A $.05/square foot		
× 1,200,000 square feet	$ 60,000	
Category B $.30/square feet		
× 200,000 square feet	60,000	
Category C $.05/square foot		
× 100,000 square feet	5,000	
Category D $.25/square foot		
× 12,500 square feet	3,125	
Category E $.05/square foot		
× 250,000 square feet	12,500	
Category F $.25/square foot		
× 4,000 square feet	1,000	
Lima Company aggregate bid	$141,625	

Mike Company

Category A $.075/square foot		
× 1,200,000 square feet	$ 90,000	
Category B $.145/square feet		
× 200,000 square feet	29,000	
Category C $.10/square foot		
× 100,000 square feet	10,000	
Category D $.15/square foot		
× 12,500 square feet	1,875	
Category E $.13/square foot		
× 250,000 square feet	32,500	
Category F $.18/square foot		
× 4,000 square feet	720	
Mike Company aggregate bid	$164,095	

Based on the four competitive bids received, the Lima Company was selected as the Ten-Twenty Corporation term painting contractor for calendar year 1989, with a low aggregate bid of $141,625.

CASE STUDIES AND SUGGESTED SOLUTIONS

What Is Required

Formulate your responses to the following questions:

1. Do you agree with the selection of the Lima Company for the 1989 painting term contract? If you do agree, state why.
2. If you do not agree that Lima was the best selection, explain why. Should some other company have been selected? If so, which one and why?
3. Given the particulars of this case, does the possibility of fraud concern you? Explain.
4. If you believe that fraud is likely in this case, do you believe that conspiracy may be involved? Explain. Name the "players." Be specific.

For Your Guidance

For the purposes of this exercise you may ignore the possibilities of fraud that could arise as the result of duplicate payments, double payments, and defective deliveries.

Suggested Solution

Note: In analyzing this case please bear in mind that the amounts and circumstances have been cast in such a manner as to make them more or less self-evident. Those in an actual case would be more likely to be subtle and subdued, and much less evident.

This case is a relatively realistic version of the fraud type previously described as involving unbalanced contract bidding, which can take a wide variety of forms. In this instance the successful painting contractor is the Lima Company, which was selected for its low aggregate bid of $141,625 (versus bids of $166,720, $171,490, and $164,095. Actually, if the bidders were held to the quantities of painting specified in the Request for Proposal's specified painting categories A through F, the Lima Company's $141,625 offer would have clearly been the proper selection. Ironically, anyone viewing the selection process in its early stages would be very likely to concur.

As a matter of fact, were the Lima Company required to perform painting in accordance with its bid offer, it would very likely lose money. What it has done, however, is "unbalance" the line items in its bid in such a manner that two purposes are served:

1. The aggregate bid is sufficiently low to assure the contract award for the Lima Company. This is done by submitting prices for certain line items that are ridiculously low.
2. Unit price bids proposed for certain categories of painting are abnormally high, assuring Lima of excessively high profits *if* those painting categories were to be selected by the Ten-Twenty Corporation to the exclusion of painting categories priced abnormally low.

Consider, for example, the following comparison of unit prices offered by the four bidders:

Unit Prices by Category

	A	B	C	D	E	F
Lima	.05	.30	.05	.25	.05	.25
Average of other bidders	.08	.15	.10	.15	.12	.18

Note that the Lima Company's prices are very low on painting categories A, C, and E, and very high on painting categories B, D, and F. Consider what their profits would be were the Ten-Twenty Corporation to *not* require any painting in categories A, C, and E, but order large requirements of painting in categories B, D, and F.

Were the Lima Company to unilaterally presume that it would not have to deliver painting categories A, C, and E as stipulated in the Request for Proposals, it would be extremely foolish, indeed. Rather, they have the assurance of an inside conspirator that it will not be called upon to do so. The inside conspirator further assures Lima that the offices to be painted are in such bad shape that only categories B, D, and E painting (two coats) will be required, and very likely in quantities in excess of those stated in the RFP. In fact, the inside conspirator is not only in a position to know these things, he is also in a position to make them happen.

With regard to your responses under "What Is Required," you should have answered:

The Lima Company was a good selection *provided* the RFP line items were all required in the quantities stipulated for price proposal purposes. However, you had every reason to believe that the contract would not require the line items specified, in the quantities specified. For example, the RFP stipulated that "no minimum or maximum painting requirement" would be stated in the contract, and "the Ten-Twenty Corporation may at its option increase any of the painting requirements, without limitation, at the unit prices offered and accepted."

If you agreed that the low aggregate price was an adequate reason for selecting Lima, you would be very vulnerable to the fraud that appears about to occur. However, in your defense, were you to object to the selection of the Lima Company before the fraud occurred, in a real-life situation you would be speculating that fraud was intended and, in effect, recommending that a higher bidder be selected. Quite possibly, if all the bids were made public, the Ten-Twenty Corporation could be exposed to criticism—and possibly litigation—for not picking the low bidder. After all, it is difficult for you to know with certainty that the Lima Company would lose money, and there is no law preventing the Lima Company from submitting a "loss" bid, for whatever reasons it may have. Perhaps Lima feels that it wants to "buy in" on profitable future contracts.

If you did not agree that the Lima Company was the best selection, for the reasons we have already discussed, you were correct. Proving your conclusion, however, may require a circuitous path. By this we mean that rather than simply expressing your opinions, the irregular bid particulars *should be regarded as indicia of fraud*, and your observation should be kept confidential.

Assuming that you are an auditor with access to records, using the indicia that you have discovered, you should proceed on the contention previously discussed in Chapter 5, that the thief involved is unlikely to have committed only once the crime you suspect. Accordingly, assuming that the crime of fraud has occurred, and that an inside conspirator must be involved, determine who that inside person, or persons, is likely to be. Once having determined that, your task is to review other transactions that have occurred in the past in which that person was a key player, and which also displayed irregular circumstances, possibly involving unbalanced contracts.

Depending on your findings, a course of action should be obvious. If you find no other instances in which similar irregularities have been noted, we can only recommend that you very carefully consider your comments in a case like this. Unless you have been very lucky in your evidence disclosures, it is not likely that you could convincingly defend an allegation of fraud, even though there was no doubt in your mind. In this instance, you would probably have to restrict your comments to retroactive observations that "Lima Company may not have been the best choice" or that "Ten-Twenty managers were unwise in deviating from the painting category quantities published in the RFP."

CASE 7. THE ARCHIVE

For Your Information

A previous section of this book mentioned a variety of fraud called "reopened competed contracts." This case involves one of these.

Many entities rely upon "competed" contracts to protect their interests. The belief is that the marketplace, composed of many independent bidders, will (1) produce a competitive and fair price, and (2) prevent an inside conspirator from "rigging" a contract and assuring its award to an associate. This belief is naive and, in fact, often achieves just the opposite of what was intended. That is, the competed contract is often manipulated in such a manner that its award to an associate is assured, at a price often considerably above that available in a free and unmanipulated marketplace.

This is a brief hint of what you are expected to look for in the following case. Once again the case is presented simply, without complicating details, for improved understanding.

The Situation

In 1988 a fire in one of the Bluebird Corporation's makeshift storage rooms destroyed a sizable number of important records. The irreplaceable loss motivated the corporation to proceed with plans to acquire a centralized storage facility suitably designed to preserve its records efficiently and safely. It was also decided that the facility acquired would be large enough to store the documents and computer back-up records from all of the corporation's entities.

Tom Logan, chief architect of Bluebird's architectural office (AO) was directed to design a suitable facility and to estimate construction costs. Two months later Tom submitted a preliminary building design and his $3 million cost estimate for the new structure, including estimated land acquisition costs.

Shocked by the cost estimate, the board of directors unanimously rejected it as too expensive, directing instead a search for an existing building that could be purchased and modified, if necessary, for substantially less cost.

Several options were under consideration, all of them discouragingly expensive, when it occurred to the search party that an existing Bluebird-owned warehouse would be ideal for the records storage site. Warehouse #3 had been substantially unused since 1967, following its use as a storage facility and shipping terminal during the Vietnam war years, when Bluebird had geared up its La Crosse manufacturing facilities to support military contract production. However, it was acknowledged that extensive renovation would be necessary to convert the site into a suitable records storage facility. Nevertheless, its use was advantageous in that (1) the facility would be located on Bluebird's premises, assuring convenience and security and (2) the elimination of the need to acquire a basic structure and its underlying land would provide a first-class archives structure at a reasonable price.

The search team submitted its recommendation to use the Bluebird vacant warehouse #3, and Tom Logan submitted his renovation design together with an estimate that it would require approximately $1 million to accomplish the renovation. The completed archive would be a first-class facility. The Bluebird board quickly approved the recommendations and directed that the project be started as quickly as possible.

Tom's design required the following major renovation features:

1. Construction of a security vault to accommodate sensitive documents; the vault and archives storage areas to be air-conditioned and have humidity controls. (*1*)

138

2. The use of twin 48-inch fluorescent lighting fixtures through-out the storage building. (*1*)

3. The resurfacing and leveling of the existing concrete floor, which was badly cracked and uneven, with a 4-inch minimum concrete veneer. (*1*)

4. The removal of old combustible exterior siding, and the installation of brick veneer on the entire outer surface of building. (*1*)

5. The resurfacing of interior walls and provision of partitions in accordance with specification drawings. (*1*)

6. Installation of ceilings in accordance with specifications provided. (*1*)

7. Installation of 165° fire-suppression water sprinkler heads throughout structure, as specified. (*1*)

Note (1): All features portrayed in detail on Bluebird blueprints were provided with Invitation for Bid (IFB) packages mailed to all interested contractors.

On July 17, 1989, the Bluebird construction engineer's office issued an Invitation for Bids (IFB) to several large contractors who had expressed an interest in doing the job. They were required to submit sealed bids on or before 12:00 noon, September 17, 1989. The job requirements, including a complete set of blueprints prepared by Tom Logan's architects, were included in the IFB package sent to each contractor.

Upon bid opening on September 17, it was disclosed that the low bid of $711,000 had been submitted by the Acme Builders, of La Crosse, Wisconsin. The Acme bid was rejected, however, in favor of a bid of $1,003,500 submitted by Baker Contractors, Inc. The reason given for rejecting the Acme bid was their failure to name the sub-contractors who would be used on the job, a stipulation required by the Bluebird IFB.

The contract was awarded to the Baker firm, at its bid price of $1,003,500. The contract included a value engineering (VE) incentive clause, standard on all Bluebird construction contracts, that offered the performing contractor an opportunity to share half of all cost savings that he was able to achieve by recommending cost-cutting improvements in contract specifications. However, all changes were subject to Bluebird approval.

The two other bids received were $1,126,999 and $1,245,987.

The Baker Company made excellent progress on the renovation project. By September 30, only three weeks after they had started work, they were well ahead of schedule. The old interior structures of the building had been cleared away, and most of the old exterior siding had been removed.

On October 19 it was discovered that two errors, or omissions, had been noted in the contract requirements that had been distributed with the IFB package. The contract was changed to correct them.

Change 1. A Bluebird consulting archivist/architect discovered that the contract specifications required 165°F sprinkler heads, as opposed to the 286°F heads recommended for records storage. The 165° heads were undesirable, because in the event of a small fire the sprinklers would be activated at the relatively low fire temperature of 165°, resulting in significant water damage, even though the fire damage might be quickly controlled. Baker Contractors, Inc., were directed to make the change, and the contract price was increased $3,120 to include the cost of changing to the 286° sprinkler heads.

Change 2. The consulting architect also discovered that the renovation specifications provided that the warehouse doors at each end of the building be built 48 inches in width. The width was insufficient to accommodate the Bluebird Corporation's material handling equipment and pallets. Contract specifications were changed to provide for 96-inch wide entrances at both ends of the building. The price for installing two new doors was estimated at $3000 each, or $6000 for the two entrances. Since the brick veneer had already been installed, no credit was allowed, and an additional $5000 was estimated as the cost of removing the new brick veneer and finishing the door openings to the new specifications. The contract was changed to provide for the change, and to increase the contract price $11,000.

Change 3. The consulting architect also discovered that the Bluebird specifications mailed to the renovation contractors failed to include an air-conditioning and humidity control system, essential to records and computer media storage. The change was particularly expensive because of the need to provide an extensive air delivery system, as well as the cooling/humidifying equipment itself. Baker estimated the cost at $125,000. Contract Change 3 was written to provide for it.

Change 4. In addition to the three contract changes described, a fourth was requested when the Baker people noted that the lighting fixtures required by the contract were not normally used in archive facilities. The basic contract provided that twin side-by-side 48-inch fluorescent fixtures be installed throughout the storage area. Baker pointed out that single-tube, 96-inch fixtures are preferred for records storage facilities. Reporting that the single 96-inch tubes would reduce contract cost by $35,000 because fewer fixtures would have to be installed, Baker received a $17,500 VE bonus for recommending the savings which were approved by Bluebird. In recommending the change, the contractor cited a standard requirement for federal and other records storage areas located throughout the country which provided that light fixtures for stack areas be "fluorescent, continuous strip (single tube) not more than 9 inches wide including the maximum width of the reflector." The contract price was reduced $17,500 to reflect one-half of the Bluebird saving. Change 4 was written to provide for VE lighting change.

Change 5. The Baker contractors also advised that the new concrete floor, which was a required contract specification, was unnecessary. They recommended that an asphalt-based paving material be used instead. The asphalt surface was priced at $87,000. The cost of the concrete surface which had been included in the contract was $125,000. The VE savings would be $38,000, $19,000 of which would be Baker's share under the value engineering clause. The change was approved by Tom Logan, and the contract price was reduced by Bluebird's share of the savings, or $19,000. Change 5 was written to provide for the VE change in floor materials.

The renovation contract was completed on March 3, 1989, and shortly thereafter Bluebird began erecting tall metal shelving structures to hold the many boxes of records soon to come. The Baker renovation work was inspected by Tom Logan personally on March 5, and the performance under the terms of the contract was approved as highly satisfactory. A check was issued to Baker Contractors, Inc. for the following:

Basic contract		$1,003,500
Contract Change 1	+	3,120
Contract Change 2	+	11,000
Contract Change 3	+	125,000

Contract Change 4	–	17,500
Contract Change 5	–	19,000
Amount of check		$1,179,120

Ten months after large sections of shelving had been erected and loaded, the metal supporting columns began to sink into the relatively soft asphalt floor. This created a dangerous situation resulting from the likelihood of loaded shelving units (weighing about 2500 pounds) toppling over. Eventually another contract with Concrete, Inc. was entered into to replace the asphalt surface with concrete. A structural engineer with Concrete, Inc. stated that in his opinion asphalt was not strong enough to support the weight of fully loaded shelving and should not have been used for the job. No attempt was made to get the Baker company to correct the problem without charge, because Tom Logan stated that he was responsible for approving the asphalt floor-surfacing material used. In fact, Tom was not at all as alarmed at the prospect of the shelving toppling over as was Ann Cestor, the Bluebird archivist. Tom stated that shelves uniformly loaded would not become unstable until the top reached a lean of at least 30 inches. He continued, saying that the farthest lean measured so far was only 3 inches. To Ann Cestor's concern over the "domino effect" Tom replied that it was unlikely, since the aisles were 30 inches wide and shelving units leaning toward each other would form a sort of tepee and stabilize. Ann did not ask why he assumed the shelves would lean together.

What Is Required

Carefully consider all of the details provided, then prepare a list of questions that occur to you, with regard to the basic contract itself and the Contract Changes 1 through 5. This case has been modeled after an actual case, but has been simplified for presentation here. Do not list the sort of fraud possibilities that have been discussed in Cases 1 through 6.

Suggested Solution

As briefly described in the introduction to Case 7, this case study deals with the rigging of a competed contract to defraud the contracting victim. *Normally*, a rigged contract involves (in this order):

CASE 7. THE ARCHIVE

1. A conspiracy between a bidding contractor and an employee of the victim who can influence contract administration or supply vital inside information.

2. The preparation of contract bid specifications which are deficient in some subtle way.

3. A low bid by the conspiring contractor, probably a loss bid, which assures the lowest price bid and, very likely, the contract award.

4. Contract specification changes, usually initiated by the inside conspirator, to correct the built-in deficiencies and allow the contract to be repriced at exorbitant profits. Note that the contractor "anticipating" the changes can save even further by minimizing or eliminating salvage expenses—but still charge for them.

In the Archive Case, the first question that confronts the alert investigator is that of the low $711,000 bid submitted by Acme Builders. In the actual case, the low bidder was eliminated for the same reason stipulated, that is, that it failed to name the subcontractors it planned to use. One might ask, is this sufficient reason to eliminate a bid that was almost $300,000, or 30% less? Particularly if it was the only reason? In the actual case that this was taken from, it was the *only* reason. Further, assuming that it was a valid concern of the contracting company, it is interesting to note that in the real case, the second-lowest bidder that was awarded the contract (as was Baker Contractors in this case), although listing the subcontractors that it intended to use (a bidding requirement), were never required to use those subcontractors and, in fact, never did.

In retrospect, it appears that the Acme bid was a good bid, but for some unexplained reason failed to provide the names of its subcontractors. How then do we explain the three bids that were in relatively close proximity around $1,000,000? What may have happened is that the two high bidders offered their bids in a conspiracy with Baker Contractors to make it *appear* that there *was* competition and that the Baker bid was a bona fide low. Although it is illegal, sometimes dishonest contractors do conspire with each other to "rotate" available construction business without cutting each other's throats. Nevertheless, we do not know what happened here, but the alert auditor or investigator would question the above observation.

In this case study, what had happened was that Tom Logan, Bluebird's architect, designed certain deficiencies into the building renovation specifications to provide the subsequent opportunity to amend the contract and defraud his employer.

Consider Change 1, which provided that the fire sprinkler heads be changed. An additional $20,000 was allowed to the Baker firm to remove the 165°F heads and install the 286°F heads. As a matter of fact, there are *two* frauds rolled into one here. In the first fraud, theoretically, Baker included a sum in its basic price proposal to install the 165°F sprinkler heads as required by the specifications. The fact is that the existing warehouse already had the 165°F degree heads installed, and their rated life was far from expired. The second fraud is that when it was asked to provide a price for making Change 1, Baker claimed that it had already installed the 165°F sprinkler heads (when they had not), and hence their Change 1 price offer included no credit for work eliminated. In fact, the price included the cost of removing the 165°F heads that they allegedly had just "installed."

Consider Change 2. The "discovery" that the end doors were not wide enough came as no surprise to Tom Logan. It was planned. As such, the renovation work was planned so as to accommodate the wider doors and to not require any removal of work already delivered under the original contract. Of course, when Baker was asked to prepare the cost of making the necessary change, it claimed that work had progressed to the point that delivered work would have to be removed before the new doors could be installed. Naturally, Baker's price proposal for Change 2 was provided long after the new work had been done, which provided no risk that anyone would accidentally discover their progress at that point.

No credit under the original contract was possible, and Baker would have to be paid to remove the new construction in place.

As for Change 3, needless to say the air-conditioning and humidity control systems were not overlooked. They created an undeniable opportunity for reopening the contract and submitted inflated prices.

No explanation is necessary for Change 4 at this point. The Baker people give the Bluebird Corporation "an opportunity" to *save* $17,000.

Finally, consider Change 5—another opportunity to save money. Substitute asphalt instead of concrete and save $38,000. This one backfired, however, and the soft asphalt floor failed to support the heavy steel shelving used to store the Bluebird records. The failure actually caused the contract's administration to be reviewed and, in the process, brought the other items into question.

In the actual case that this was taken from, there were many more items, including more dollar-significant items, that were involved in the fraud.

CASE 8. THE MORTGAGE

The Situation

You are an auditor reviewing the loan portfolio of the Sundown Savings and Loan Association. You have been reviewing loans for three days when you come to a $125,000 loan secured by an office building located at 12345 Old Orchard Road. You review the loan file and note that the loan, made on July 1, 1988, was recommended and approved by Harvey Goodfellow, president and chief executive officer of Sundown.

Upon further review of the loan file, you note that the Old Orchard Road building had been appraised by the Sundown appraiser at $140,000. You note too that the appraisal was based on the prior two sales of the building. It was sold in November 1987 for $135,000, the new owner apparently taking a quick profit by selling it again in March 1988 for $150,000. The current owner, who borrowed the $125,000 to purchase the building, paid $160,000.

What Is Required

Comment on the foregoing. Do you think that Sundown made a good loan? As auditor, you check out the facts stated above and find them to be correct. Is there anything else that you would ordinarily consider doing in your investigation?

Suggested Solution

This is actually a very simple case, but because of the degree to which it was used in the recent savings and loan scandals, we thought it worth including for those few of you who may not have heard of the practice.

What is involved here is something that has come to be known as "land flips." Land flips have been around for a long time, but seem to have come into their own during the savings and loan scandals of the late 1980s. However, the practice is hardly limited to savings and loans. It happened as long ago as about 1960 in Chicago, when the lower value of a building was "flipped" upward until it justified its sale to the government for about $14 million. Actually, any product, from diamonds to art objects, can be flipped to make an inflated asking price appear reasonable.

Flipping involves the contrived sale and resale of an item, for instance, a building, between conspiring partners for the purpose of falsely inflating the item's value. With each sale the price is increased and further increased. When it is finally sold to a third party or used as collateral for a loan, the last sale price is far in excess of its actual value. This happens because it is customary for appraisers to look to recent sales as a point of reference in estimating value. Often there is little other reference as to an item's value other than "the price someone has been willing to pay for it"—in other words, the marketplace.

In Case 8, you are made aware that the building sold in November 1987 for $135,000 and was sold again for $150,000 in March 1988. From these figures it would appear that the last sale price of $160,000 is not too far out of line. In addition, the loan at about 78% of its value does not appear to present too great a loss exposure. What was *not* determined in the loan file was that the building was purchased in July 1987 for $50,000, and there is no legitimate evidence that it is worth any more than that.

For those who may be interested in reading actual examples of land flipping on a grand scale, the following book is recommended: *Inside Job* by Stephen Pizzo (McGraw-Hill, 1989). The book describes actual cases in which properties were flipped to increase their sales/loan value. It tells of one instance (p. 46) in which a property was deeded back and forth several times in one afternoon to increase its apparent value from the $40,000 purchase price to secure an $80,000 loan. In another instance (p. 22) it describes how a piece of property was acquired for $4 million, then sold back and forth to increase its value to $40 million.

9

COMPUTER FRAUD

No text on the topic of fraud would be complete without a discussion of computer fraud. Its treatment here will be restricted, because any significant coverage could easily be a textbook in itself. The following news item appearing in *The Wall Street Journal* (November 22, 1988) is worth noting:

> HIGH TECH SUCCESS: Thieves working with computers steal an average $500,000 each time they strike, dwarfing the average $23,500 taken in all white-collar crime and the $250 grabbed in armed robberies, Brigham Young's W. Steve Albrecht tells a Peat Marwick conference.

There are several good reasons that automated accounting systems tend to facilitate fraud. The principal reason may be the impersonal functioning of the computer.

Microcomputers are available to practically every level of a company's operations, from top management to sales, from bookkeeping to maintenance. Furthermore employee use of microcomputers to work off-site is commonplace. One does not have to be an employee who is familiar with the company's operations to gain access to data process files. Horror stories of maverick hackers appear almost weekly in *The Wall Street Journal* and other national business publications.

Because of the highly technical nature of computer-based fraud, we will address only the management accountant's perspective on computer fraud. As with other technical cases of fraud, it may be in the best interest of management to involve computer experts if computer-based fraud is suspected.

Although we are often dazzled by the data-processing capabilities of computers, we must keep in mind that they are only machines that blindly process data at extremely high speeds, in languages foreign to most observers. They cannot discern whether the data being processed is true or false, nor can they discern when they are a party to fraud. Computers do not have a sense of right or wrong as do their human counterparts. In short, they can be manipulated by *anyone* having access to them, and they will obey a manipulator's instructions to the letter.

AREAS OF VULNERABILITY

Computer systems are considered to be vulnerable to fraud or misuse in several key areas. The AICPA *Audit and Accounting Manual* cites many of these areas of vulnerability and suggests possible controls to offset the inherent risk:

1. The computer department functions are not fully segregated from users. For example, a using department may create source documents, enter them into the system, operate the computer, and produce output. This environment poses risks such as deliberate concealed errors, unauthorized master file changes, inadvertent input errors, and lost or corrupted data. Some controls to offset these risks include transaction and batch control logs, independent review of logs, use of passwords and other access supervision, rotation of user duties, requirement that master files be altered only with applications programs that generate an internal log of all changes made and by whom, and periodic comparison of vendor programs with the company's version.

2. The location of computers in the user's area gives rise to the following risks: unauthorized use of data files, unauthorized modification of programs, misuse of computer resources. Controls suggested to offset these risks include password-protected menus, periodic review of usage history reports, and physical control over the system hardware, such as locks and read-only terminals.

3. Lack of computer department segregation of duties presents the following risks: unauthorized access to master files and programs, concealment of deliberate errors, and programs that are not representationally faithful to management's objectives. Controls to mitigate such risks include limited access to source code, periodic comparison of programs in use with authorized program versions, password protection to limit access to an as-needed basis, and management review of logs.

4. A lack of technical computer knowledge by computer supervisory personnel raises potential risks such as the inability of a supervisor to recognize failure to meet management objectives and the inability to test and review the system effectively. Controls to offset these risks include use of documentation and checklists and recruitment of outside personnel to review program modifications.

5. Use of utility programs that bypass the system log to make master file and program modifications leads to several risks: unauthorized access to data and programs, undetected changes to files, and processing and concealment of unauthorized transactions. The primary means to control these risks are to require all program and master file modifications to be made through the relevant application program and to limit access to system utilities.

6. Diskettes pose a variety of risks because of the relative ease of concealment resulting from their size and data capacity. Risks include processing the wrong data files and bypassing error logs. Controls include restricted access to the control diskette library and the use of read-only terminals.

7. Terminals are located throughout the company premises and offsite, which poses the risk of unauthorized access and unauthorized data entry. Controls include read-only terminals, terminals that can access only certain programs and files, and the physical security of hardware and access logs.

8. Readily available vendor software encourages suboptimization of management objectives. This happens because users find it more convenient to use programs that are already familiar to them, even though such packaged software may fall short of management objectives. Such programs are often not tested by authorized personnel before they are used and accepted. About the only control over this risk is to require that all user-acquired software be tested by system personnel to ensure that it complies with management objectives.

EXAMPLES OF COMPUTER FRAUD

Perhaps one way to heighten one's sensitivity to the problems that can be created by the use of computers, especially now that microcomputers are readily available to company personnel, is to survey several examples of computer crimes that have been perpetrated.

1. Officials of a bank in Los Angeles discovered that an employee had used the bank's computer to embezzle $21.3 million dollars, the largest electronic bank fraud in U. S. history at the time of its occurrence.

2. An individual in California stole $10.2 million dollars from Security Pacific Bank with one telephone call. The perpetrator gained access, through a ruse, to the wire transfer room at Security Pacific Bank. While in the room, he was able to obtain three vital pieces of information:

a. The security number used to authenticate each day's transfer orders. This code is changed daily.

b. The personal code used by one of the bank's security officers to identify himself to the system.

c. The account number of an account that had a large balance on deposit.

With this information he was able to initiate the wire transfer of $10.2 million dollars from the Security Pacific Bank to a bank in Zurich, Switzerland. The bank did not discover that the $10.2 million was missing for approximately two weeks.

3. An insurance company bilked financial institutions of millions of dollars through the creation of fictitious policies that were subsequently used to collateralize large loans to the insurance company.

4. A senior employee in the bookkeeping department of a local bank, over a period of six years, embezzled over $250,000 and concealed the embezzlement through false entries into the bank's computer system.

5. An employee of a large New York bank programmed the bank's computer so that when computing interest on customers' accounts, every fraction of a cent was credited to the employee's personal account.

6. Seven workers at a state welfare office in Miami were convicted of stealing $300,000 in negotiable food stamps by falsifying data fed into the agency's computer.

7. A company bilked $190.4 million dollars from 19 lending institutions. They were induced to purchase notes secured by false leases. In purchasing the notes, lenders were led to believe that the notes were secured by valid and binding leases, and that payments on the notes would be made from rentals of data processing equipment due each month under the terms of the leases. In most cases the equipment did not exist. However, in others, the equipment was found not to be leased or records were altered to reflect higher rentals.

The following are commonly employed business security measures:

1. Strictly controlled access to the computer room and the central processing unit.
2. Access through remote terminals limited to information retrieval only.
3. Segregation of employee functions, such as data entry, operation, programming, and system analysis.
4. Periodic review of data processing security.
5. Supervisory review of all program modifications and changes.
6. Frequent unannounced audits of computer outputs.
7. Requirement that all data processing and accounting employees take annual vacations.
8. Security codes for access to both the computer room and computer terminals, particularly those in remote locations.

EXAMPLES OF AUDIT TESTS

Several years ago U. S. General Accounting Office auditors made a study of the controls in a federal agency's automated payroll system. They found system weaknesses which, they believed, if exploited, would result in fictitious payroll checks. To test their theories, without the knowledge of the system's operators, they provided the necessary input they believed would generate a payroll check to a fictitious employee named Donald Duck. It worked. With check in hand they reported the weaknesses and provided recommendations for strengthening the system. Management reacted by minimizing the auditors' finding, saying that "when the check was handed out, someone would have noticed Donald Duck's check and would have caught it at that time."

In another interesting example, auditors in the U. S. General Service Administration's Kansas City Regional Office were reviewing a national purchasing and inventory control system when they noticed that a number of important internal controls were missing. They believed that the system was vulnerable to fraud. However, from prior experience they were aware that the system's designers were fiercely proud of their system, were thin-skinned, and would be hard to convince that the system needed to tighten.

After considerable internal debate, the GSA auditors decided to attempt to exploit the weakness, to prove their findings on internal control. Before doing so, however, they took pains to disclose their plans to the agency's law enforcement staff, to assure that their actions were never mistaken for a serious attempt at fraud—which could otherwise very easily happen. Incidentally, this kind of disclosure is a must for anyone who may someday attempt to exploit a system weakness to prove that the weakness exists. That is, *be sure to disclose your test to someone of trust, who can be depended on to verify your intentions should something go wrong.*

For the test, a purchase order was prepared ordering 96 general mechanics tool kits at a cost of $97,200 from the General Tool Company, a fictitious vendor. An unsecured computer terminal was used to establish that a purchase had been made and to signal the automated system that stock was due in. Thirteen days later a computer terminal was used to notify the automated system that the 96 tool kits had been received. Six days later, on June 18, the auditors created an invoice for the phony tool kits, billing the government $97,200 for them and offering a 2% prompt payment discount if paid in 20 days. The company's mailing address was P. O. Box 17732, Kansas City. On July 5 a government check for $95,256 was mailed to Box 17732, the auditor's post office address. From the government's Kansas City computer terminals, another fictitious order for tool kits to be sent to the government's depot in Ft. Worth was also successful.

Obviously, the automated systems most vulnerable to fraud are financial payment systems. They include, primarily, payroll systems and those disbursing regular monthly annuities. The so-called computer frauds, however, are not necessarily a product of the computer era. They were present in payroll and annuity disbursing systems that existed prior to the computer era, which means that you do not necessarily have to be a computer expert to find them.

In a case that occurred before the large-scale use of computers, a large insurance company utilized metal plates to mechanically imprint monthly annuity checks each month, to be mailed to annuitants. As you may surmise, someone had slipped a few extra metal plates into the imprinting machine, causing checks to be mailed to nonexisting annuitants. In today's computer age metal plates are no longer used, but in lieu of plates their data equivalents can be surreptitiously inserted into a computer's master file of payees. Since many of these disbursement systems are on an exception basis, i.e. once the data is in the file no other action is needed to cause additional checks to be issued, fraudulent disbursements would continue without interruption for a long period of time.

VARIATIONS ON A SCHEME

It is impossible to give a complete and comprehensive picture of the many ways to commit fraud in a cash disbursing system in this relatively brief guidebook. However, consider some of the following possibilities:

1. In an annuity payment system, annuitant Jones dies. The death notice is mailed to the paying organization. Employee A of that organization intercepts the death notice and substitutes a change-of-address notice. Future checks are mailed to her address.

2. In an automated payroll system employee Jones leaves the company. Employee A delays the termination order and changes the mailing address, perhaps for one or two checks.

3. Employee A has the opportunity to input fictitious annuitants or payroll names into the computer.

To prevent the foregoing, at the very least you are advised to

1. Carefully review the data input controls of the automated payment systems, with the intention of reducing the opportunities for inserting false data into the master payment records.

2. Have an ongoing program for selectively reviewing actual input. One of the controls that every automated system should have is a record of *every* change to the master record. The processing program should provide for it. The changes may be serially numbered to make tampering more difficult and should be available in a format that can be used by auditors—on paper for smaller systems, or microfilm for larger systems.

3. Review all changes to program software.

4. Always presume that someone has found a way to compromise the controls. Have an ongoing program for selectively test-checking outputs.

Normally, audit efforts should be clearly *visible for their deterrent value.* There are literally countless things that a computer audit program can do to protect system integrity. Every system is different. Protective measures are limited only by your own creativity.

10

INVESTIGATING
SUSPECTED FRAUD

The purpose of this chapter is to provide the fraud auditor with fundamental investigative procedures. Although the investigation of violent crimes differs in many ways from investigation of white-collar crimes, particularly fraud, there are many commonalities.

Top management has overall responsibility for an organization. Therefore, although this chapter is addressed primarily to fraud auditors, it also aims to be informative for progressive top managers who are interested in learning about the activities of a very important control element of the organization, fraud auditing.

Because of the auditor's strategic position within the company, he or she will often be the first person to arrive at the "scene of the crime." At a minimum, the auditor is often the first person to become aware that a crime may have been committed. The following material introduces the fraud auditor to principles and technique used by professional investigators. Perhaps more important, the material will provide fraud auditors with information designed to assist them in preserving and documenting facts about a suspected fraud and its suspected perpetrator. The facts preserved by the fraud auditor will assist both in the accumulation of evidence and in the prosecution of the perpetrator if prosecution becomes appropriate.

An investigator collects the facts and lets the facts "tell" whether a crime has been committed and who committed the crime. The object, sometimes ignored by investigators, is to make the shoe fit the foot and not vice versa.

An investigation begins with the discovery of a possible crime. There will be times when something initially appears to be the result of sinister criminal activity when, after all the facts are gathered, is determined to be simply the result of mistake, ineptness, or incompetence. Conversely, there will be times when suspects will encourage the investigator to believe that activities that are criminal in nature are only the results of mistake, ineptness, or incompetence.

The purpose of an investigative plan is to allow the investigator an opportunity to determine how to attack the problem in an organized manner. The investigative plan takes into consideration the following factors:

1. *The crime.* What are the elements of this crime and what information must be collected in order to prove those elements?

2. *Materials.* What types of materials will have to be reviewed to prepare the investigator and properly investigate the crime? Is there a "crime scene" that may contain physical evidence? Are there documents to be reviewed? Is there a process about which the investigator will have to learn (for example, chemical plant production, silver futures, sawmill operations)?

3. *Witnesses.* Are there witnesses available? What are their relationships to the crime and the suspect, if there is a suspect? In what order should they be interviewed?

CASE ASSESSMENT

The first component of the investigative plan is to make an assessment of the case. This requires the investigator to evaluate the situation in terms of threat, risk, and vulnerability.

Threat. Anything of value has some kind of threat to it. For example, if we live in a high-crime, inner city neighborhood, the threat of being mugged is considerably greater than if we live in a small, close-knit farming community in the Midwest. We can identify the threat of being mugged by simply understanding that muggings more likely occur in certain types of areas, at certain times of day, and if we exhibit certain types of behavior.

Risk. Risk is the likelihood that a threat will occur to the object we are investigating. Certain banks, for example, have a higher risk factor because of where they are located. They are *more likely* to be robbed than other banks because of their threat factors (for example, isolated location, location adjacent to a convenient escape route, generally known periods when large amounts of cash are present).

Vulnerability. A facility may have a high threat and high risk quotient, but have low vulnerability because of other factors. The bank in the isolated location with known periods of high cash presence may be so heavily guarded and have such stringent security measures that its vulnerability is very low.

The investigator must then make a list of the threat, risk, and vulnerabilities within the situation. This defines the parameters of the investigation. For example, if a situation is threatened, at risk, and vulnerable only to a certain group of persons at a certain time, it limits the initial population of suspects and witnesses and defines the kind of manpower required to resolve it. A simple example is the difference between losing a five dollar bill in downtown Chicago around noon on a weekday and trying to figure out who picked it up, compared with the theft of $1000 from a company safe between 4:00 P.M. and 5:00 P.M. when only two persons could have had access to it. In the first case, investigation would be meaningless from a standpoint of the value of the loss and from the possibility of identifying the person who picked up the five dollar bill. In the second case, the investigation would be very focused, require low manpower expenditure, and probably be resolved within a short period of time.

INTERVIEWING

The investigator's main tool is the interview. All interview techniques should take into consideration a number of common factors.

Nothing in the ordinary experiences of growing up prepares us for the process of obtaining accurate information from sometimes very reluctant people. The investigator must overcome his or her own reluctance to be insistent or to "pry" into certain areas.

In normal society, people voluntarily tell things that reflect their moods, make them seem important to the listener, cause the listener to react in a certain way, or optimize their own positions. People rarely volunteer information that is detrimental to their own self-interests.

In many crimes such as fraud, conspiracies, and other white-collar crime, the interview is often a significant means of collecting the facts needed to make the case. The reason for this is that people may agree verbally to commit certain bad, or corrupt, acts but rarely reduce such agreements to written form. Witnesses observe not only written acts, but a whole gamut of activities, including physical activity (Bill opening the safe drawer), associations (Joe and Bill always eat lunch together), conversations (I heard Joe tell Bill to open the safe), and other occurrences that cannot be readily initialed and placed in a file by the investigator.

There are essentially two general methods of influencing the state of mind of witnesses and suspects. The first is physical or mental abuse. Of course, this method is completely unjustified and illegal in our society and under our laws.

The second method predominantly consists of systematic interviewing conducted in a humane and friendly atmosphere. The inhibitions of the person being interviewed are replaced by logic, and any natural incentives to cooperate are stimulated to the point that the individual feels that truthfulness will be beneficial in some way.

Personal Attributes of the Interviewer

Four of the most important qualities of an interviewer are

1. *Honesty, integrity* and the ability to impress upon all interviewees that the investigator seeks only the *truth*.
2. *The ability to establish rapport* quickly and under a variety of conditions.
3. The ability to *listen* to interviewees and evaluate their responses to questions.
4. The ability to *maintain self-control* during interviews and not become emotionally involved in the investigation.

It is the investigator's job to convince the interviewee to divulge information. In this respect, the investigator must keep in mind several guidelines, which reflect attitude and personality, and avoid the obvious traps.

1. Do not prejudge a suspect or witness.

2. Subdue all personal prejudices regardless of whether they are social, racial, sexual, or of any other type.

3. Keep an open mind, receptive to all information regardless of its nature.

4. Try to evaluate each person and each piece of information on its own merit.

5. Do not deliberately lie or make false promises to an interviewee.

6. Refrain from trying to impress the interviewee unless such action is specifically part of an interviewing technique.

7. Do not underestimate the mental ability of the interviewee.

8. Avoid contemptuous attitudes.

   a. Do not ridicule.

   b. Do not consider success a "victory" but simply the accomplishment of the interview objective.

   c. Do not bully. Remember that the person being interviewed is there at his or her leisure, not the interviewer's. The interviewee can get up and leave anytime he or she desires.

   d. Keep all promises.

   e. Do not belittle the interviewee, his or her situation, or his or her information.

   f. Avoid controversial matters to the maximum extent possible (for example, religion, politics).

   g. Be fair.

9. Avoid creating the impression that the only thing of interest is a confession or a conviction.

10. Do not shout or raise your voice unless it is absolutely necessary as part of a practiced, proven technique.

11. Always maintain control of the interview. The interviewer is there to obtain information and therefore must remain in charge.

12. Be serious about what you are doing. You can display warm, personable confidence and still maintain the seriousness of the situation.

13. Be a good listener. The investigator's job is to learn, not to impart information.
14. Be patient and persistent. You will rarely get what you are looking for early in the interview. Keep at it until all of the information available is obtained.

People and Their Personalities

Generally, interviewees may exhibit any or all of the following characteristics:

1. They have faulty perception.
2. They have faulty memories, which vary in direct relationship to the amount of time that has passed since the incident.
3. They do not know what it is you want from them.
4. They are generally reluctant to get involved.
5. They are not impressed with authority; they may hate authority; they may hold a grudge against authority; they may be fearful of authority.
6. They may have been intimidated by the suspect; they may be loyal to the suspect; they may be related to the suspect.
7. They do not want to be inconvenienced.
8. They have faulty logic.
9. They mistake inferences for facts.
10. They have differing levels of mental capacity, mental health, and intelligence.
11. They conceal or distort information for personal reasons.

Questions and How to Ask Them

If questions cannot be understood by the interviewee, the information you seek will not be forthcoming, or will be inaccurate.

When composing questions, you must take into consideration the background of the interviewee. Persons of different ethnic, educational, and social backgrounds will have differing vocabularies. As a rule, the simpler a question the better. You must be sure that you understand the words and manner of speech of the person being interviewed. Local idioms ("of a morning," meaning A.M.), uncommon words ("croaker sack," meaning a burlap bag used in frog hunting), trade expressions ("two ten net thirty," meaning deduct two % if paid within 10 days, otherwise total amount due within 30 days"), regional accents ("hit were," meaning "it was") and imprecise sentence construction ("He ain't lie from nobody," meaning "He would not lie for anyone") can result in a misunderstanding unless the investigator makes sure that the words are completely understood. When asking a person to explain one of these matters, ask, "What do you mean by . . ." as opposed to, "Do you mean . . .", since people often will agree with an investigator just to agree (because of the investigator's authority or because the interviewee thinks the investigator understands).

A question is used to persuade the listener to make a predictable topical response. If the questioning process is not carried out properly, it may confuse, irritate, or intimidate the listener, thereby reducing the flow of information.

Good questions have identifiable characteristics regardless of the topic:

1. Good questions are short, simple, and confined to one topic. (Where were you on August 12, 1988, at 2:30 P.M.?) Do not use complex sentences. (Did you go to the bank and kill Mary, or eat dinner?)

2. Good questions are clear and easily understood. (What color is your car?)

3. Good questions avoid sensational words. Avoid using such words as *confession, drug addict, doper, stool pigeon, drunkard, child molester, rapist, embezzler.* Try to use milder terms that do not evoke strong emotions.

4. Good questions are precise. Do not ask, "What did you do?" when you mean, "What did you do about getting to the meeting last Thursday night at about 7:00 P.M. when your car had a flat tire on Route 29?"

5. A good question requires a narrative answer. A question that results in a yes or no answer is usually a leading question and can result in a restriction of the information received by the investigator.

The Six Basic Interrogatives.   *Who, What, When, Where, Why,* and *How* are the six basic interrogatives. If you start each question with one of these words, you will not be asking a leading question since each requires a narrative answer rather than just yes or no. Some schools of thought also include the interrogative *Which.* Couple the characteristics of good questions with the six basic interrogatives and you have the foundation of the interview.

Question Sequencing in Interviews.   All things in a person's life happen in a chronological order. People are generally comfortable relating a story in a chronological order. Jokes, stories, movies, and the other information we share in daily life generally presented are in chronological sequence.

One of the problems with interviews is that the interviewee is being asked to describe an activity that took place in the past. The investigator should be aware that memory is *reconstruction*, not *recollection*. It is sometimes useful when asking questions to frame them in such a way that the interviewee can use a time-related reference point for such reconstruction (for instance, a birthday, a holiday, another significant event).

In using the *general-to-specific questioning technique* the interviewer guides the interviewee from the general to the specific. It involves a narrowing of time-related information to a specific instant or event. The general-to-specific technique aids the witness in information reconstruction and can trap the suspect in a story that is difficult to change once he or she sees the ultimate direction the interview is taking.

In moving from point to point, try to use a transition to connect the thoughts. Phrase a transition question by using known information to proceed to the unknown. If the interviewee has a good grasp of the information, but is simply having trouble phrasing it properly or keeping it in sequence, the investigator might ask, "What happened next?" or "What did you do next?"

Another technique, *the controlled answer questioning technique* is used to stimulate an interviewee to agree to talk or to give information. For instance, the interviewer might ask, "Since you were not involved in this situation, you won't mind answering a few questions, will you?" The technique can also be used to stimulate a suspect to acknowledge certain critical facts, which may ultimately result in a confession. For instance, the interviewer may ask, "Eddie and others have told us that you were at the bar on Thursday night with Mary, so you're not going to deny that, are you?" This is a stronger question than "Were you at the bar on Thursday night?"

Three Main Parts of the Interview

The interview consists of three main parts: free narrative, direct examination, and cross-examination.

Free narrative is a continuous account of an event or incident that is given with a minimum of prompting by the investigator. Its purpose is to get the witness talking and to obtain a quick resume of what the interviewee knows. Remember, you will get only what the interviewee wants to tell you or what he or she thinks you need to know. The free narrative has the effect of involving the interviewee completely in the interview and overcomes any initial objection to providing a detailed reply to a question.

One problem with free narrative is that many people digress or get sidetracked on issues that are immaterial to the investigation, but may be important to the interviewee. Do not be too hasty to jump in and try to redirect the narrative. Give the interviewee a little room to wander, because valuable information may come up in an unexpected context. However, once you see that the digression is not leading in a meaningful direction, politely interrupt and steer the interviewee back to the point where he or she left the trail. If the topic of the digression subsequently assumes importance, at least you know about it and can reinterview for more detail if necessary.

When beginning the direct examination, start off with the soft, easy questions so as not to alienate the interviewee. People will answer difficult questions a lot sooner if they have been talking to the interviewer for a while than if they are asked difficult questions pointedly without a warmup period.

When asking questions, do not be in a hurry. Remember to have patience. Everyone thinks and arranges information at a different speed. After you have talked with the interviewee for a while, you will know whether he or she is stalling or whether it just takes the person that long to answer a difficult question.

There will come a time when you will have to help an interviewee remember. It is important not to suggest an answer or imply that any particular answer is preferred over another. If you have information that might be helpful in assisting the person to remember, divulge it a little at a time until the person reconstructs the information in his or her mind.

If a person seems confused, repeat the question after having rephrased it. Work with the question until the interviewee understands it and gives you an answer.

If an interviewee uses terms like "we," "I heard," "He told me," be sure to determine just exactly who "we" and "he" are. Be sure to find out whom he or she "heard" it from. Be aware of persons using as their own the thoughts, sights, sounds, and facts learned from another. Obtain specific detail when dealing with interviewees. Some people are very accurate about time-distance relationships, others are not.

The final phase of an interview is the cross-examination phase. At this point the investigator has listened to the free narrative and filled out all the blank spots through direct examination.

Discrepancies in the responses of interviewees, and even of suspects, may be the result of error as well as evasion. Cross-examination is designed to reconcile that problem. Cross-examination will usually address certain specific areas where there are significant discrepancies in information. Clues to those areas include

1. Attempts to evade answers. Be particularly alert if a person starts to answer your question and then goes on to tell you about something else. This usually indicates that he or she is trying to avoid answering your question.
2. Vague answers.
3. Conflicts of information.
4. Inconsistent answers to the same or similar questions.
5. Apparent lies.

Change the contextual matter of the question. For instance, the first time you might ask, "When did you first meet Joe?" Then you might later ask, "What were you doing when you first met Joe?" You might follow with, "What led up to your first meeting with Joe?" "Did you know Mary when you first met Joe?" "Who knew Joe first, you or Mary?"

Ask about known information as if it were unknown, and vice versa. If the investigator's delivery is smooth and casual, the interviewee will not know what the investigator knows and what he or she does not know. However, be careful about trying to bluff an interviewee, because the interviewee might just call the bluff.

When conducting a cross-examination, it is important to have first obtained as complete an explanation as possible from the interviewee. Ask all necessary questions before any confrontation, because the interviewee, upon being confronted with discrepancies, may terminate the interview.

A fourth aspect of the interview, if required, is the confrontation. This is the point at which the discrepancies are placed before the interviewee and an explanation is requested. This is a critical point in an interview. This is when you are essentially telling a person that he or she is either lying to you or just doesn't understand what he or she is talking about. Few people suffer through this moment easily. Continue to be patient and persistent, requesting an answer to the conflict. Do not let the interviewee off the hook without a resolution.

NOTE TAKING

Investigator's notes are critical and deserve special attention. The content of the interview notes will determine the success of the investigation. These notes are the basis of all reports and, ultimately, the prosecution.

During the interview, the investigator should take careful notes of what is being said by the interviewee. Where possible, the investigator should use the exact words of the interviewee. These notes, made at the time of the interview as the words are being spoken, are called *contemporaneous notes*.

There is no specific format for note taking. They should be written on a standard 8½ by 11-inch lined notepad. This type of notepad will also be useful if a statement has to be taken.

As a general guideline, notes should be written so that another person, unfamiliar with the investigation, could read them and make sense of them. Do not let the interviewee rush you and force you to take less than adequate notes.

At the beginning of the interview, the investigator should write at the top of the first page of the notes the following information concerning the interview and the interviewee:

1. Date, time the interview commenced, place of interview.
2. Full name, position, work and home addresses, work and home telephone numbers of the interviewee.
3. The names of any other persons present (other investigators, attorneys, supervisors, union stewards) and full identifying data regarding these other persons.
4. Anything unusual about the circumstances of the interview (for instance, the interviewee's physical condition, such as obvious injuries).

When the interview has been completed, the investigator should review his or her notes for completeness before excusing the interviewee. After a typewritten report is made, using the contemporaneous notes, the notes should be placed in the case file in the event that they are later needed.

Notes are typewritten into a form called a *memorandum of interview*. This is simply an easier to read form of the contemporaneous notes. There are, however, several important guidelines in regard to the memorandum of interview:

Make sure that there is nothing in the memorandum of interview that is not also in your contemporaneous notes. It would be very embarrassing to be accused on the witness stand of adding information to the memorandum that was not given at the interview.

The memorandum should contain any useful narrative material indicating physical actions that took place. For example, if a document was shown to the interviewee, that document should be completely described in the report at the appropriate place.

The investigator's personal opinions, conclusions, or noninterview-related observations should *never* be placed in the body of the memorandum of interview.

WRITTEN STATEMENTS

There will come a time in every investigation when the investigator will have to take a written statement. This statement is taken for the purpose of preserving the testimony of an interviewee. A statement should be taken only when, in the opinion of the investigator, it is absolutely critical. A statement is taken at the end of the interview after the investigator has obtained all the information from the interviewee. Although there may be exceptions, most persons are willing to put in writing what they have just told you orally. If you ask a person about a written statement before the interview is complete, he or she may decide to withhold information or become reluctant to cooperate.

Every statement, regardless of format, has certain common characteristics. The beginning of the statement, usually the first paragraph, should contain identifying data about the person giving the statement (for example, name, address, date of birth) and an acknowledgement of what the statement concerns (for instance, "I am giving this statement in connection with an investigation into the theft of $5,000 from the company safe"). In addition, the fact that the statement declarant can understand the statement should be included (for example, "I can read and understand the English language").

The next and all succeeding paragraphs should be directly applicable to the investigation, and each paragraph ideally should cover one topic. An example follows:

I arrived at work on January 14, 1989, at 9:30 A.M. When I arrived at Smith and Associates, Incorporated, there were three other people already at work. Those persons were Mary Wade, Betty Compton, and Larry Boswell. When I walked into the office, I noticed that the safe door was open and the inside of the safe was empty.

The statement could then go on to describe the declarant's activities and other information in subsequent paragraphs.

After all the relevant information is written into the statement, there should be a concluding paragraph. This paragraph should be an attestation on the part of the person making the statement that the statement is true, accurate, and obtained under legal circumstances. A typical closing paragraph might look something like this:

I have read this statement consisting of this page and two other pages. I have given this statement freely and voluntarily without any threats, reward, or promises of reward having been made to me in return for it. It is true, accurate, and correct to the best of my knowledge and belief.

The interviewee should carefully read the statement and initial any corrections that have been made. The object of taking a statement is to obtain information that cannot be changed at a later date should the interviewee be intimidated or bribed, or simply think better about becoming involved.

The statement should be typed or neatly handwritten. The usual practice is for the investigator to write the statement in the interviewee's presence, while the interviewee watches.

Statements serve several purposes. They can be used to refresh a witness's recollection. They can be used to impeach a witness who changes his or her story at a trial. They can be used to elicit information from reluctant witnesses. (People would rather be part of a group in doing something like this than doing it alone.) They can be used as leverage with suspects to demonstrate that information has been obtained from other sources that supports the investigator's suspicions of guilt.

Sworn Statement

A sworn statement, or affidavit, is a statement taken from an interviewee before a person authorized by law to administer oaths. This authority is statutory in nature.

If a sworn statement is to be taken, the person authorized to administer the oath should swear in the interviewee before the signature is placed on the document.

The person giving the oath should then write in the *jurat*, or the authentication line. This is usually a line that states: "Subscribed and sworn to (or affirmed) before me this 27th day of March, 1989, at Chicago, Illinois" (the appropriate date and location being placed in the proper places). This is then followed by the signature of the oath-giving individual.

In our system of government, more reliance is placed on sworn testimony than is placed on unsworn testimony. This does not mean that an unsworn statement is useless, since it is adopted by the person giving it with his or her signature. The least desirable statement is one that is unsigned and unsworn.

CONTACT WITH THE PROSECUTOR

Question-and-Answer Statement

Question-and-answer statements, or "Q and A" as they are called, are verbatim statements. The Q and A shows the exact questions asked and the answers given. This type of statement is taken when the answers of the interviewee are critically important and a narrative answer will not be suitable.

The body of a Q and A statement looks like this.

Q: What kind of weapon did Joe have that night?

A: It was a revolver.

Q: What make of revolver was it?

A: It was a Smith & Wesson .38.

CONTACT WITH THE PROSECUTOR

A prosecutor should be contacted when fraud is first discovered and the victim intends that the crime be prosecuted. Each prosecutor has different preferences with regard to the evidence needed to support prosecution. Different criminal statutes may apply and require different sorts of substantiating evidence to be gathered. Also, some prosecutors may be more demanding than others in their evidenciary requirements. For example, one U. S. Attorney who we had worked with, after successfully prosecuting a case of fraud had this admonition for us the *next time around*. He advised us that if possible he would prefer documentation of more than one instance of fraud by the accused, as was the case in the evidence package we had provided to him for prosecution. He had been concerned that the one example would be insufficient, regardless of it's significance, to clearly convince the jury that the defendant had clear intent to defraud. His concern was that juries sometimes tend to be overly sympathetic to a plea by a defendant's attorney that *one instance of fraud does not a criminal make.*

Also, prosecuting attorneys often have varying degrees of investigative resources that may be available to assist in evidence gathering. U. S. Attorneys, for example, probably have the most investigative resources available because they have every federal law enforcement agency (there are over 80 of them) at their disposal. Prosecutors at state, county, or equivalent level however, are not as fortunate, and may depend more heavily on the victim's resources to accomplish any necessary investigative activities.

SUMMARY

The fraud investigator must patiently and persistently accumulate information to be used in the decision to prosecute a perpetrator, as well as in an actual prosecution of a fraud perpetrator. Interview questions should be phrased in such a way so as to elicit a narrative response. The interrogatives Who, What, Where, When, How, Why, and Which are useful in asking such questions.

The end product of the fraud investigator's efforts may be a memorandum of interview or a signed statement. In either case the document should be supported by legible and complete notes taken at the time of the interview. These notes may be presented as evidence during a fraud trial. Their content, clarity, and consistency is of the utmost importance if the prosecution is to have a reasonable chance to secure a conviction.

11

RULES OF EVIDENCE

The rules which determine what constitutes relevant and substantive evidence in establishing the existence of fraud and perpetrator guilt, are of paramount importance. The courts and its officers are well versed in them, and fraud cases presented for their considera tion must be in conformance. Oftentimes, however, the rules of evidence are voluminous and written in a 'legalese' which is difficult for the layman to understand. It was with this concern in mind, with apologies to our lawyer readership for any *liberties* taken, that the following text explaining the rules of evidence was written for our non-lawyer accountants and auditors who are reading this book.

The rules of evidence are complex and have been the subject of hundreds of books and essays. The material that follows presents an outline to facilitate finding summary information quickly. The wording has been "delegalized" to the extent possible without denigrating the meaning of the context. As it is most likely, once evidence of fraud is discovered, that competent legal counsel will be called in to guide the evidence-gathering process, this chapter is not intended to be a substitute for such counsel. It is rather intended to guide the management accountant and internal auditor, those who are most likely involved in fraud discovery and control efforts, in completing their training and education on the topic of fraud discovery and control.

The ultimate decision to prosecute a suspected perpetrator of fraud must be made by top management either as a matter of policy, (preferred by the authors) or on a case by case basis. All cases of suspected fraud should be documented as if it were the intent of top management to prosecute the perpetrator. Therefore, no discretion to prosecute or not to prosecute the suspected perpetrator of fraud is given to the management accountant or auditor within this text material.

Successful prosecution of fraud depends on the relevance and materiality of the evidence and, most important, whether the preponderance of evidence is valid beyond a reasonable doubt. Therefore, internal auditors and accountants can greatly assist the prosecution of fraud by ensuring that there is substantial documentation of fraudulent transactions. The information that follows is intended to provide the reader with general information related to evidence and evidentiary rules which should be considered in identifying, documenting, and confronting fraud within various entities.

The detection, documentation, and prosecution of fraud require vigilance and strong commitment on the part of all managers, executive staff, and employees of a company. Since a perpetrator could be anyone, including a valued and long-time employee, identification and confrontation should take place if and when there is clear and convincing evidence. Such evidence should, on its face, be non-speculative, but rather should point to the loss of property and the fraudulent conduct of the employee(s) in question. Once the individual is detected and successful prosecution is achieved, the entity must follow through with its own internal sanctions, which may range from suspension and probation to restitution and termination. The culminating action of the entity should include preventive systems changes to ensure that opportunities to commit similar fraud have been eradicated.

WHAT CONSTITUTES FRAUDULENT CONDUCT?

Solicitation

Modern statutes refer to criminal behavior that solicits another person to commit a crime. Solicitation may also constitute criminal attempt when the crime was one requiring joint action of both parties; for example, soliciting another to give perjured testimony is punishable as a criminal attempt to perjure oneself.

Conspiracy

Conspiracy is an agreement between two or more parties to do an unlawful act or to do a lawful act in an unlawful manner. A defendant could be prosecuted for conspiracy as well as the completed crime. For successful prosecution, an agreement between two or more persons, either expressed or implied, must be proven.

Two or More Persons. In *Gebardi v. U.S.* (USSC, 1932) the facts were that a man and the woman he transported were charged with a conspiracy to violate the Mann Act. The man made all of the arrangements; the woman voluntarily consented to go with him.

Congress intended by the Mann Act to exempt the woman of the substantive crime. Therefore, the woman could not be convicted of conspiracy to violate the Act. Since she is not guilty, neither can the man be guilty, since *it takes two persons to commit a conspiracy* (there must be an *agreement*).

The Model Penal Code would convict the man in the *Gebardi* case. That is, it says, if you agree with someone to commit a crime, you are guilty of a conspiracy even if the other person is not. Most courts, however, follow the *Gebardi* rule.

In *Regina v. O'Brien* (Canada, 1954)—*one party without the requisite intent*, the facts were that A and B agreed to a kidnapping, but A never at any time had the intent to go through with it. A *could not be held since he did not have the requisite mental state accompanying the commission of a prohibited act (mens rea).* The issue uses whether B, who did intend to commit the crime, was guilty of conspiracy.

In this case the defendant was found not guilty because there was not the requisite meeting of the minds between two or more people to conspire to commit a crime.

Under common law a husband and wife were considered to be one legal person and could not, therefore, conspire with one another. Many courts have now rejected this view. If, however, husband, wife, and a third party agreed to commit a crime, then there is a conspiracy and all are guilty.

False Pretenses/Misrepresentations

False pretenses consist of obtaining title to personal property of another person by an intentional false statement of past or existing fact with intent to defraud that person. A misrepresentation as to what will occur in the future is not sufficient. A false promise, even if made with the present intent to perform, is also not sufficient.

The victim must actually be deceived by, or act in reliance on, the misrepresentation, and this must be a major factor (or the sole cause) of the victim's passing title to the defendant.

Larceny by trick consists of obtaining possession of personal property (with the intent to deprive) by a misrepresentation of past or future fact; *false pretenses* requires that the defendant obtain title. Whether the victim transfers possession or title depends upon the victim's intent.

Robbery

Robbery consists of taking personal property of another from the other's person or presence (including anywhere in his vicinity) by force or threats of immediate death or physical injury to the victim, a member of his or her family, or another person in the victim's presence, with the intent to permanently deprive the victim of his or her property.

Extortion (Kickbacks)

Under common law extortion consisted of the corrupt collection of an unlawful fee by "an officer under color of his office."

Under modern statutes, extortion often consists of obtaining property by means of threats to do harm or to expose information, or merely of making threats to do such things with the intent thereby to obtain property. Modern extortion covers several situations not covered by robbery:

1. Where the threats are not of the required physical harm or of sufficiently immediate harm, or
2. Where the property obtained is not in the victim's presence.

Receipt of Stolen Property

Receipt of stolen property consists of receiving possession and control (manual possession of property is not necessary) of personal property, knowing it to have been obtained in a manner constituting a criminal offense by another person with the intent to permanently deprive the owner.

Theft

Under many modern statutes, some or all of the above-mentioned property offenses are combined and defined as the crime of *theft*.

Forgery

Forgery consists of making or altering (by drafting, altering, adding, or deleting) a writing (defined as a writing with apparent legal significance) so that it is false (defined as representing that it is something that it is not, not as merely containing a misrepresentation) with intent to defraud (although no one need actually have been defrauded).

If the defendant fraudulently causes a third person to sign a document which that person does not realize he or she is signing, forgery has been committed. But if the third person realizes he or she is signing the document, forgery has not been committed even if that person was induced by fraud to sign it.

Uttering a forged instrument consists of offering as genuine an instrument that may be the subject of forgery and is false with intent to defraud.

Malicious Mischief

Malicious mischief consists of the intentional destruction of or damage to the property of another. Malice requires no ill will or hatred. It does, however, require that the damage or destruction has been intended or contemplated by the defendant.

·Embezzlement

Embezzlement consists of fraudulent conversion of personal property by a person in possession of that property where the possession was obtained pursuant to a trust relationship.

Note: If the defendant intended to restore the exact property taken, it is not embezzlement. But if he or she intended to restore similar or substantially identical property, it is embezzlement, even if it was money that was initially taken and other money—of identical value—that he or she intended to return.

As in *larceny*, embezzlement is not committed if the conversion is pursuant to an open claim of right to the property.

Embezzlement differs from larceny in that

1. Embezzlement can be committed only by one with valid possession of the property (although if he had mere custody, larceny can be committed).
2. Embezzlement requires only fraudulent conversion, rather than taking and transportation.

ELEMENTS OF CRIME

The three elements of a crime are *actus rea, mens rea, and causation.*

1. *Actus Rea* is either the commission of some act which is prohibited by law, or negative acts, or omissions to act. If an individual omits some act where there is a legal duty to perform it, the individual is criminally liable (for example, cover-up).

The essence of the *actus rea* is that the facts derived must point to the defendant's commission of a prohibited act under the law (for example, taking money without permission or knowledge of the owner, thus defrauding the owner).

On the other hand, mere omissions to act, if proven, could establish criminal intent and liability, especially where the individual had personal knowledge of the fraudulent act and conduct, provided assistance, was a coconspirator who provided minimal or some assistance but did not receive any of the benefits from the fraudulent act.

2. *Mens Rea* is the mental state accompanying the commission of an act prohibited by law. The defendant's mental state must have been specific intention to defraud or commit a crime.

The *mens rea*, or mental state, of the suspected individual is critical to establishing that a crime has been committed. In most fraud cases *mens rea* will be easily established by clear and convincing documentation that points directly to the actions, behavior, and control of the property in question in the hands of the suspected employee. Thus, if someone gave the employee permission to borrow or use the property for a period of time, the requirement of intent to defraud will not be easily proven in this instance.

3. *Causation* means that the defendant must have actually caused the result before he or she can be held criminally liable for the crime. Additionally, according to the *material factor rule*, it is necessary that the facts indicate that the actions and behavior of the accused were materially responsible for the commission of the fraud. In the instance of causation of the fraud, under the general rule of *res ipsa loquitor* (the act speaks for itself), the property which was defrauded was under the control of the suspected employee(s), and this property could not have disappeared without their knowledge and control over its disappearance. Thus it is essential to prove carefully through material evidence that the suspected individual had full control over and access to the defrauded property (for example, because the defendant had the keys to the safe or was responsible for counting the bonds each day, he should know about the loss of the contents.

PROCEDURES FOR DISCOVERY

It is of the utmost importance that the following factors be taken into consideration when applying fraud discovery procedures:

1. *Wiretapping and other forms of electronic eavesdropping* are prohibited by the USSC. However, the defense must prove physical invasion or trespass to limit the admission of information obtained by such means. We recommend that a court order first be obtained. In *Rathburn vs. U.S.* it was ruled that an employer can listen to any conversation that is conducted during the course of business on the employer's premises.

2. *The use of a private investigator to obtain incriminating statements (evidence)* is permissible. In *Osborn vs. U.S.* it was ruled that tape recordings might be admissible under certain circumstances.

3. In *Baggio vs. U.S.* (1987) *informants* were permitted to be used to admit evidence gathered. It is essential that the agency/employer consider a court-appointed informant, or an informant from the U.S. prosecution or local state attorney's office. The other option is an individual competent to undertake such an operation, such as a private investigator.

4. Internal *auditor's reports* are excellent documentary proof of fraud. In most instances an internal audit will be required after the suspicion of fraud, or in the normal course of a regular audit if the internal auditor uncovers a fraudulent act.

5. *Confrontation* is permissible in some instances in which there has been probable cause that directly links an individual's actions to a suspected fraudulent conduct. The suspect could be confronted about such suspected fraud. It is suggested that such confrontation be conducted in privacy with as few people present as possible. In all instances it is important to have two people perform the confrontation to ensure that there will be at least one available witness to the statements of the suspected individual.

6. *Confession*, under the rules of evidence, could be admitted as a *hearsay declaration against interest*. However, there are careful steps that should be followed in documenting an individual's confession to a suspected fraud.

a. The individual should record in writing or on tape that the statements are being made voluntarily, willingly, and without any threats or coercion.

b. The entire confession must be in writing or recorded fully.

c. The text should be signed and dated by the declarant.

d. The parties to such a statement should witness it or at least note in a separate document that they were present and that the statements were voluntarily given and duly signed by the declarant whose confession was witnessed.

Another option available to the employer is to turn the matter over to the company's internal security personnel and let them secure the confession. Since these are trained law enforcement individuals, they will follow appropriate procedures for securing a confession from the accused party.

7. *Coercion* may be used by the employer to gather vital information from an employee suspected of fraud, by threatening to suspend or fire the employee. This method should be used carefully until and unless the employee is charged with fraud or there is substantial proof of such fraudulent conduct.

Other methods may be used by the employer whose establishment is experiencing losses as the result of fraud. Any legitimate method can be used to gather information in order to detect, document, and apprehend an individual suspected of fraudulent conduct. The decision as to when to involve outside sources, such as private investigators or law enforcement officials, would in some cases determine the types of strategies that are ultimately used.

It is important that the strategy or procedure used to detect fraud should cause as little disruption as possible to the normal operations of the business enterprise. Since in most fraud the scheme is carefully contrived, an investigation should proceed without giving notice to the suspected individual(s) that they are under surveillance and that their conduct and transactions are being monitored.

EVIDENCE

Relevance in Documenting Fraud

The documented facts concerning the alleged fraud should meet two legal evidentiary tests; namely, it must be logically and legally relevant.

1. *Legal relevance* refers to whether the evidence has probative value, and is presented in a fair, unbiased, clear manner that will enable the trier of the facts to understand and rely on it.

2. *Logical relevance* refers to any evidence that will have the effect of making the existence of a material fact relevant to the issue more probable than it would without the evidence.

There are several recurring questions as to the relevance of evidence presented:

RULES OF EVIDENCE

1. Liability Insurance. The courts have consistently held that evidence of liability insurance is not sufficient to prove malfeasance or misfeasance. This evidence of liability insurance basically will show that an individual has ownership of such insurance. Therefore, the limited admissibility of this evidence will be to show control and ownership of the liability insurance only.

2. Subsequent Changes. Evidence of subsequent changes and other precautions made by an employer following a fraudulent act are inadmissible to prove negligence or culpable conduct on the part of the employer. However, it may be admissible to prove ownership or control, to rebut the claim that the precaution (against the fraudulent act) was impossible. Additionally, this evidence might be useful in proving that the accused party had damaged the internal security of the operations, which resulted in the need for such subsequent changes.

3. Settlement Offers. It should be noted that offers to compromise and settle a matter of fraud are not admissible to prove that the fraud was committed. Therefore, withdrawn guilty pleas and offers to plead guilty are not admissible. Some courts, however, have allowed admissions of facts which accompanied offers to pay restitution for the injured party's losses resulting from fraud.

4. Similar Acts. The evidence of any previous similar conduct, or acts resulting in fraudulent conduct, of the parties accused or of other persons in the same department, may be relevant if the evidence is probative of (substantiates) the material issue involved.

Specific types of similar acts include the following:

a. *Previous tort claims.* Evidence that the party has made previous similar "false" claims is considered relevant under a common scheme or plan theory, to prove intent to defraud.

b. *Previous similar deliberate acts by a party.* Similar evidence of conduct committed by a party (such as suspension or firing for similar fraud) may be introduced to establish that there was a motive or intent, when such motive elements are relevant.

c. *Prior contracts and course of conduct.* A prior agreement of conduct between the accused and the employer may be admissible to show that the accused party was aware of the proper and acceptable course of conduct.

d. *Habit evidence.* Under federal rule (406a) "evidence of the habit of a person . . . is relevant to prove that the person's conduct . . . on a particular occasion was in conformity with the habit."

e. *Evidence of industrial or business routine.* Any evidence that will show the norms and standards of care and established business routines is relevant and admissible to show that a particular event occurred.

It is essential that the internal accounting standards and business procedures be fully understood by the internal auditor or other investigating parties. The documentation of fraudulent action and conduct will involve a full discussion of the variances and conformities to the business or industrial standards of conduct and care.

Real Evidence and Fraud

The issue of real evidence is important in the documentation and prosecution of fraud. *Real evidence* is the actual physical evidence that will be presented in court to prove that the conduct of the accused party was in violation of a criminal law related to fraud. The critical issue here is authentication of the real evidence. The discussion that follows is intended to provide the reader with practical requirements that assist in the authentication of real evidence.

The following are specific kinds of real evidence:

1. Reproductions and Explanatory Real Evidence. This type of evidence includes photographs, diagrams, maps, models, charts, pictures of accused, and other reproductions. These are admissible if their value is not outweighed by the danger of unfair bias and prejudice to the accused party. However, it is necessary to ensure that these reproductions are authenticated through testimonial evidence that they are faithful reproductions of the objects they depict.

2. Jury's view of the scene. The trial court in its discretion may permit the jury to visit the scene of the crime to view the conditions and circumstances surrounding the alleged criminal conduct.

3. Demonstrations. The court in its discretion may permit experts to demonstrate or conduct experiments to amplify the conditions and circumstances related to the criminal conduct.

Documentary Evidence

Documentary evidence, such as an audit report or forged checks, must be relevant to the charges in order to be admissible. In the case of such written documents it is generally viewed as only one aspect of the proof that a particular fraudulent act has been committed.

The courts continue to be consistent in their ruling that writings or other documents will not be received in evidence unless they are authenticated by proof that clearly shows that the writing or document is what the proponents claim it is. The appropriateness or relevance of the writing or documents may be admitted into evidence by the stipulation of the parties or in the pleadings.

Evidence of authenticity may be gained in a particular audit report or document by the following means:

1. *Direct evidence*, which includes the following:

a. Testimony of an eyewitness to the actual execution of the writing or document, or to the commission of the fraudulent act.

b. Handwriting verification of the document by a handwriting expert.

c. Any evidence that the accused party has either confessed, admitted to its authenticity or acted upon the writing as though it were authentic, with the intent to commit and carry through with the fraudulent act.

d. Testimony as to the authenticity of the writing or document or the fraudulent act, by any person who can prove personal knowledge of the accused person's fraudulent action. For example, if a supervisor personally signed the checks for fraudulent invoices prepared by the accused party and under the signature of the accused party, such first knowledge of the fraudulent invoices would be admissible.

2. *Self-authentication of documents* refers to the fact that some documents and writings "prove themselves." These documents include:

a. Certified copies of public records.

b. Official publications.

c. Trade inscriptions.

d. Newspapers and periodicals.

e. Acknowledged documents.

f. Commercial papers and other related documents used in the normal course of business.

g. Published guidelines and operational procedures of a company.

3. *Circumstantial evidence* may consist of a writing or document, which may be authenticated by any of the following:

a. Evidence that the writing is a written response to a communication sent to the claimed other author. This rule is called the *reply letter doctrine.* There is an analogous doctrine that is applied to telephone logs and telephone messages.

b. Evidence that the writing is an "ancient document" (at least 20 years old under the Federal Rules of Evidence." There is some further clarity needed here because under federal rules all writings apply, whereas in most jurisdictions there is limited admission of ancient documents to such items as wills and deeds.

A final note on authentication: the "best evidence rule" should be adhered to in most cases. This rule, more accurately called the "original document rule" requires that the original writing and fraudulent documents must be produced if the terms of the proposed fraudulent act or documents are to be material and reliable as evidence of the facts purported.

The exceptions to the production of the original document include the following:

1. Duplicates or photocopies are admissible if authenticated or certified by an official person (for example, the auditor) as being a true copy of his or her audit report.

2. The writing is admissible if it is collateral to the litigated issue. The essence of the writing is of little importance to the matter in controversy.

3. The writing is admissible if the fact to be proven has been authenticated independent of the particular writing.

4. If it can be proved that it would be inconvenient to examine a voluminous collection of writings in court, the proponents may present their contents in the form of a chart or summary.

5. Photocopies of public records are admissible. Again, efforts should be made to secure certification from the record keeper.

The proponent of secondary or duplicate copies of a writing should be prepared to provide some excuse or justification for the admissibility of secondary evidence, such as the following:

1. The original is in the possession of a third party outside the court's jurisdiction and thus not readily obtainable.

2. The original has been destroyed, mutilated, or is unavailable because it was lost or stolen. A classic example is the *North vs. U.S.* case, in which several original documents were shredded by the accused parties.

3. The original is in the possession of the opponent party who, after due notice, refuses to turn it over. In fraud cases, such originals could include bank statements, telephone logs, safe entry logs, and other business documents.

Testimonial Evidence

Competence of Witness. The auditor, accountant, or other individual is called upon to testify as a witness to shed light on the fraudulent issues being pursued. The witness's testimony normally conforms to four basic standards: the capacity to observe, the ability to recollect facts and situations, the ability to communicate things within one's knowledge and perception, and the competence to appreciate the obligation to speak the truth in response to all questions.

Opinion Testimony of Witness. The courts are not anxious to admit opinion evidence of lay witnesses unless there is proof that no better evidence can be secured. In most jurisdictions and under federal rules, opinion testimony by the lay witness is admissible if it can be shown that the evidence is rationally based on the witness's perception and personal knowledge and such testimony will be helpful to the determination of a fact at issue. The opinion of a lay witness is admissible to verify:

1. The general appearance or condition of a person.
2. The emotional state of a person.
3. Any proximity sense perception.
4. The identity of voice, handwriting, or likeness of appearance.
5. The value of his or her own services.
6. The rational or irrational conduct and behavior of another person.
7. The intoxication of another person.

Opinion Testimony by Expert Witnesses. The role of expert witnesses will continue to be expanded, as we have seen in the fraud cases involving Wall Street brokers and other individuals. The expert, like a lay witness, will be subjected to cross-examination. The opinion of the expert witness must be supported by factual and reliable evidence and based on the personal observation of the expert, facts known to the expert at the trial, or information supplied to him or her outside the courtroom or in a hypothetical situation. The expert may state his or her opinion, providing the expert can establish that he or she is

1. Qualified as an expert in the subject matter or issue at hand;
2. Familiar with the subject matter, and it is appropriate for expert testimony, and,
3. Capable and it is reasonably probable that his or her opinion or conclusion is based on the subject matter and facts presented.

The Hearsay Rule

The *hearsay rule* is important in documenting evidence for the prosecution of fraud. The Federal Rules of Evidence define hearsay as "a statement, other than one made by the declarant while testifying at the trial or hearing, offered in evidence to prove the truth of the matter asserted." Generally, if a statement is hearsay and no exception to the rule applies, then the evidence will be excluded upon appropriate objection. Hearsay statements include oral statements, writings, and assertive conduct. Under federal rules nonassertive conduct is not hearsay. But under the common-law definition of hearsay, statements may include nonassertive conduct.

Hearsay exceptions include the following:

1. *Former Testimony*, which is admissible in a subsequent trial providing the following tests are met:

a. It is shown that the declarant is unavailable at the subsequent trial.

b. The former testimony of the declarant must have been given under oath or sworn affirmation.

c. The former action must involve the same or identical subject matter and cause of action.

It is essential that all statements secured in any investigation be in writing and be *sworn* statements. There must be convincing evidence that the witness is unavailable to testify.

2. *Admission by a Party Opponent* involves a statement made or any act or conduct that amounts to prior knowledge by one of the parties to an action of one of the relevant facts being tried. It should be noted that an admission may be inferred from conduct or facial expressions.

Another aspect of admissions may occur vicariously when:

a. An admission of one partner, relating to matters that are clearly within the scope of the partnership business, is binding upon the copartners.

b. Admissions of one conspirator are made to a third party in furtherance of a conspiracy to commit a crime at a time when the declarant was participating in the conspiracy.

These statements are admissible against coconspirators.

It should be noted that vicarious admissions may not be used where a principal-agent relationship exists unless the matters were within the scope of the agency. Generally, admissions of a party are not receivable against his or her coparties merely because they happen to be joined as parties.

3. *Declarations of Physical or Mental Conditions, Excited and Contemporaneous Utterances.* There are four instances in which such declarations are admissible due to their reliability:

a. *State of mind statements* are admissible if they prove a person's intent to perform a certain action and such an action was carried out.

b. The *excited utterances* made during or soon after a startling event are admissible when such evidence shows that a startling event did occur and the declarant had firsthand knowledge.

c. *Personal sense impressions* are admissible if the individual had firsthand presence and impression of the facts.

d. A *declaration of physical condition* is admissible if it includes personal knowledge of a person's present bodily condition and is based on a spontaneous declaration. Additionally, statements of a person's past bodily condition may be admitted to show personal knowledge of the condition in question.

4. The *Business Records* exception to the hearsay rule is critical since it includes any business records such as audit reports, financial statements and business policies. Additionally, any correspondence could be admitted to show that a transaction was completed.

The general rule is that such business records will be admitted as evidence if they were prepared in the normal course of business and professional services. The records must be authenticated and, most important, the entrant (person who made the entries) must have personal knowledge of the information recorded and such recordings must have been within the duty of the entrant.

The proof of a fraudulent transaction must be linked to the time period of the alleged fraud. The maintenance of good business records of all monetary transactions or other business activities are helpful in documenting fraudulent conduct. In addition, the auditor's report forms a solid basis for identifying the existence of fraud within an entity. Any opinions as to the estimated time frame of the fraudulent conduct could be useful in subsequent investigation and prosecution.

Privileges

The prosecution of fraudulent conduct is sometimes stymied by the accused person's Fifth Amendment right against self-incrimination.

This constitutional right provides the individual with the privilege of declining to answer any incriminating or other questions, and protects him or her from being compelled to testify.

Other privileges provided to suspected individuals are as follows:

1. *The Attorney-Client Privilege* is a long standing privilege that protects the communication and work products of the attorney and client, providing a bona fide relationship exists. The client is the holder of the privilege, therefore only he or she can waive this right. Therefore, once the accused worker has engaged an attorney, communication between attorney and client will be protected under this privilege.

2. *Husband-Wife Privileges* include protection of the confidential communications between a husband and wife during a valid marriage. One spouse cannot be compelled to testify against the other in any criminal proceeding. In federal courts the privilege belongs to the witness spouse, thus the privilege must be claimed by that spouse. A general exception to this rule can be made if there is an action between the spouses and either spouse waives his or her rights.

3. *Clergymen's Psychologists' and Physicians' Confidential Communications* are privileged in many jurisdictions. The privilege, as is the attorney/client privilege, belongs to the client and can be waived by the client alone. There are, however, cases in which the court compelled the production of medical records notwithstanding this privilege. The clergyperson enjoys a stronger privilege, and courts find it more difficult to compel any disclosure of the confidential information by a clergyman. It is up to the discretion of the clergy as to what information is disclosed.

4. *Accountant and Auditor Privilege* exists to protect confidential communications and documents and is similar to the attorney-client privilege. The client may waive this privilege. There are sufficient cases to suggest that the accountant auditor-client relationship could be breached by a court order compelling the disclosure of communication and audit reports when these confidential communications are material to the prosecution of a case or amplification of a fact in issue. As in all cases, there must be a formal relationship between the parties, and the interaction and communications must have been conducted in the normal course of business.

SUMMARY

5. *Professional Journalists* generally have no journalist-client privilege; therefore a journalist can be compelled to disclose any confidential communications and information. Resistance could result in a contempt of court citation.

6. *Governmental Privileges* follow the general rule that the government can protect the identity of an informer, or official information not otherwise open to the public, by claiming a variety of privileges that include national security, governmental privilege, and privacy and freedom-of-information laws.

Business and industry should remember that the freedom-of-information and privacy laws, both federal and state, provide protection against the disclosure of any personnel records or trade and business secrets. These laws provide very detailed procedures for the prohibition against certain protected disclosures. When faced with a subpoena or request to release confidential information, it is advisable to secure legal advice on the extent of such disclosure.

SUMMARY

The documentation of evidence of fraud must be clear, convincing, and beyond a reasonable doubt. Real evidence is crucial, and the best evidence will be original documents, direct evidence of the fraudulent conduct and behavior. The auditor's role is very important in this evidentiary gathering process. The auditor must use vigilance while conducting the audit to identify suspected fraud, report it to the appropriate authorities, and stop worrying about being a whistle blower. The fiduciary and ethical responsibility of the auditor is to identify and report both suspected and actually documented fraud.

Once fraud has been identified the entity should pursue its further documentation vigorously by any means, including private investigator, legal wiretaps, informants, and careful surveillance of the suspected employee(s). When fraudulent conduct has been established and the perpetrators duly identified, it is essential for the entity to be decisive in prosecution and to begin by using suspension, probation, demotion, restitution, and termination actions. Prosecution of a fraud serves as an excellent deterrent. Merely the suspension and firing of an employee alone are insufficient to send a chilling message to other workers—that fraudulent actions will neither pay nor go unheeded. The auditor's fiduciary and ethical responsibilities require vigilance and full disclosure of fraudulent behavior. In this period of malaise and public skepticism, such as related to audits of the thrifts and savings and loan institutions, it is important that public confidence in the auditor's work be restored. To this end, fraud must be identified and reported in a timely manner.

EVIDENCE AND FRAUD CASE STUDY

John, the manager of a Western Union office, had the combination to the safe. The only other copy of the combination was sealed in an envelope at the company's main office. John had a spotless employment record for 15 years. He had received all the highest employee awards. John was in need of extra cash to pay off a gambling debt. He abstracted $10,000 from the company safe. A subsequent audit revealed that the funds were missing. John confessed to taking the money. While the company was conducting its investigation, it was discovered that Tim, a maintenance worker, had removed $300 dollars from a cash register. Tim was caught because he was the only person in the building at the time of the theft.

Instructions

1. Identify the crimes that were committed by John and Tim.

2. How would you go about obtaining the documentation that will help the prosecutor to secure convictions against John and Tim?

3. Are you convinced that all elements of a crime have been met by the conduct of John and Tim?

4. Assume you are the prosecutor. What arguments would you put forth based on an analysis of the facts and evidence? Identify all the facts with which potential evidentiary questions might be associated. Be sure to discuss the relation of appropriate evidentiary rules to these facts and to discuss what variations in the facts might affect the rule's application.

5. Assume you are the defense attorney. What arguments would you put forth based on an analysis of the facts and evidence? Identify all the facts with which potential evidentiary questions might be associated. Be sure to discuss the relation of appropriate evidentiary rules to these facts and to discuss what variations in the facts might affect the rule's application.

6. Assume you are the judge who will be responsible for hearing the facts and ruling on the case. What analysis of the facts will you be concerned with?

7. After responding to all the preceding questions, rule on the motions and the appropriateness of the application of the rules of evidence by both the prosecutor and defense attorney.

Note: The purpose of this exercise is to provide the reader with experience regarding the application of evidence and evidentiary rules to the prosecution of a case of fraud. Role-playing is also an excellent learning tool for understanding the broad dimensions of fraudulent conduct.

12

CUSTODIAL FRAUD

Because of the diversity and far-reaching nature of the fraud universe, it is not feasible to provide more than the "basic training" for fraud auditors that is included in this book. Additional books now being planned will be devoted to in-depth analyses of special fraud topics of interest to managers, accountants, auditors, and others.

Nevertheless, there is an area of fraud that is so alarming and far reaching that it was felt important to include it here. When we speak of "custodial fraud" we refer specifically to fraud that is likely to involve the enormous pools of money which have been generated as a result of pension plan contributions, general welfare plans, insurance trusts, and the like, which are entrusted to individuals and organizations for the purpose of safekeeping and investment. The funds, which frequently exceed hundreds of millions of dollars, and often involve billions of dollars, tend to present an irresistible temptation to many people. Experience indicates that there are many who are ready and willing to commit custodial-fund fraud given the opportunity. There are also many who are quite adept at creating the opportunity.

Consider first, if you will, the extensive fraud that was epidemic throughout much of the savings and loan industry during the 1980s. William Seidman, chairman of the Resolution Trust Corporation (RTC), estimated that fraud occurred in about 50% of insolvent thrifts and contributed to failure in about 40% of them.

The event that appears to have given the massive S&L fraud its impetus was the deregulation of S&Ls in 1982. Many S&Ls found themselves with enormous sums of money, both from individual depositors who were offered juicy enticements and from "brokered" deposits from pension funds and other sources, available for their almost unrestricted reinvestment, particularly in states such as California and Texas. Moreover, no investment appeared too risky for them, since any losses that they incurred were insured by the full strength and credit of the U.S. government. Many dishonest S&L operators were quick to recognize the opportunities presented to them, and the S&L fiasco was born. What is amazing is that little was done to deter their very questionable activity during most of the 1980s, much of which was very thinly disguised.

For those who may be unfamiliar with the events and circumstances that resulted in the savings and loan failures, we recommend reading the extremely informative book; *Inside Job*, by Stephen Pizzo, Mary Fricker, and Paul Muolo (McGraw-Hill Publishing Company, 1989).

This book provides a fascinating look into the history, excesses, and key events of the 1980s which led up to what, in 1990, was estimated by the General Accounting Office (GAO) as possibly costing U.S. taxpayers $500 billion.

Although the S&L scandal is past history for the most part, it does not follow that something of equal magnitude could not happen again. And it appears that a "sequel" may at this time be in the making.

PENSION, WELFARE, AND SIMILAR FUNDS HELD IN TRUST

We are admittedly not sufficiently knowledgeable to provide all of the details of the billions of dollars in the nation's trust funds that are at risk. However, the inspector general of the Department of Labor is. His semiannual reports proclaim and document a concern that appears to be going largely unheeded by the government. Should you read the recommended book, *Inside Job* on the subject of the S&Ls, you may have an unshakable sense of *deja vu*.

Excerpts

Rather than attempt to paraphrase the concern of the inspector general, we offer direct quotations from the sources indicated. Decide for yourself whether we are not again on the brink of a devastating financial catastrophe. If aggressive action is not taken immediately, recovery from this disaster may prove difficult.

U.S. Department of Labor
Office of Inspector General
Semiannual Reports

October 1, 1989–March 31, 1990

Fraud and racketeering in pension and welfare plans are not the exclusive province of labor officials or ethnic stereotypes. Today we face a new generation of racketeers disguised as attorneys, accountants, bankers, benefit plan administrators, investment advisors, and medical service providers (p. 1).

$$* \quad * \quad *$$

Skyrocketing health care costs have caused major insurance companies to all but abandon the small-employer market concluding that it represents an unacceptable risk. The vacuum of traditional group health insurance is being filled by self-funded plans commonly known as multiple employer welfare arrangements (MEWAs).

Criminal investigations have disclosed that this environment has attracted an alarming number of fraudulent MEWAs that masquerade as legitimate providers of group health coverage. Through aggressive, deceptive representations the racketeer operators of these schemes generate millions of dollars in monthly premiums from unsuspecting small companies and their employees. Structured as a modern day Ponzi scheme, the fraudulent MEWA typically pays small claims and defers major claims while dissipating revenue through a variety of embezzlements disguised as legitimate operating expenses. . . . The consequences of such fraud are tragic. Today, thousands of employees and their workers are held personally liable for unpaid medical bills even though they believed there was health coverage (p. 2).

$$* \quad * \quad *$$

The OIG continues to express significant concerns about the nation's private pension plans' vulnerability to fraud and abuse. Inadequate audit work by independent public accountants (IPAs) and a lack of effective law enforcement are the primary factors creating this climate of vulnerability.

The Employee Retirement Income Security Act (ERISA) was designed to make plan participants the first line of defense against fraud, abuse, and mismanagement by creating a reporting and disclosure system that would keep participants fully informed. Independent public accountants' financial statement audits, however, have too often failed to meet their client responsibility to plan participants to identify and disclose material violations of ERISA. Today there exists a gap between the independent public accountants' performance and expectations of the Congress and plan participants who thought they would receive clear, precise information to permit evaluation of the status and management of their plan assets.

This audit "expectation gap" in employee benefit plans also exists in other arenas as well and is a primary factor in fostering an environment conducive to fraud and abuse. In February 1989, the General Accounting Office reported that fraud and insolvencies within the savings and loan industry could in large part be attributed to the failure of the public accountants to identify and report on significant problems. The "scandalous mismanagement and rascality" causing these financial disasters were undetected by the public accountants despite the fact that the problems were recognizable . . . (pp. 3 and 4).

*　　*　　*

Typically, fraudulent self-funded MEWAs offer premiums well below the prevailing market rate for legitimate trusts and insurance companies and do so without any intention of meeting their total reimbursement liabilities. With the expectation of staying afloat for a period of time through aggressive selling and slow claims payment, these fraudulent MEWAs have become a variation of the classic Ponzi scheme (p. 43).

Case Example Excerpts

An Atlanta corporation administering the welfare plans trust for the Drivers, Warehousemen, Maintenance and Allied Workers of America Local 1 of White House, Tennessee, and the local's president were indicted on January 18, 1990, by a Federal grand jury in Atlanta on charges of making and receiving kickbacks and embezzlement. The 7-count indictment, which named four individuals and two corporations, was unsealed on January 23 after the arrests of the defendants by special agents from OLR, the FBI, the Georgia Bureau of Investigation (GBI), and the U.S. Postal Service.

The defendants are Harbor Medical Administrators of Georgia, Inc.; James Craighead, president of Drivers Local 1; Frank Buccheri, president, chief executive officer, and trustee of Omni Employee Benefit Trust of Atlanta; Catherine Steele, secretary and chief financial officer Omni Trust in Boston, Massachusetts, and Atlanta; and Southeast Group, Inc., a corporation set up by Buccheri to receive funds for himself.

Harbor Medical was a third-party administrator of Omni Trust. As a self-insured group health arrangement, Omni provides health benefits in 16 states to approximately 9,000 employees and dependents of nearly 300 companies that participate in the trust. Sherman Dixie Concrete Industries, Inc., a participant in the Omni Trust, employs approximately 100 members of Drivers Local 1 in the Nashville area.

The indictment charges that from December 1987 through November 1988, Craighead solicited and received $4670 in the form of nine payments on a new Lincoln town car by Buccheri so that the union benefit plans would continue to use Omni Trust. . . .

From about November 1987, through August 1988, Buccheri, Steele, Rowe, and Harbor Medical allegedly embezzled approximately $368,788 from Omni Trust account by taking commissions to which they were not entitled . . . (pp. 45–46).

*   *   *

Laborers District Council Building and Construction Health and Welfare Fund in Philadelphia: . . . Mims was responsible for reviewing and approving claims for medical benefits filed by eligible members of the local. From September 1985 to January 1987, she processed fraudulent medical benefits claims, causing checks to be issued to the other defendants. The checks were cashed or deposited in various bank accounts and divided among the coconspirators (p. 46).

Inspector General's Comments

October 1, 1988–March 31, 1989:

In 1987 there were approximately 870,350 private pension plans and some 4.5 million welfare plans. The private pension plans alone cover approximately 76.6 million participants, and they include assets of more than $1,600,000,000,000 ($1.6 trillion), or about $7000 for every man, woman, and child in America. This amount of funds, roughly equal to one-half the public debt, is the basis for the future economic well-being of most American workers, in their retirement. Yet *the Department of Labor's oversight of this massive amount of pension funds has been ineffective (italics added).*

. . . the Department of Labor still has only about 300 auditors and investigators to examine these funds: a number that permits the annual review of less than 1 percent of the ERISA-covered benefit plans. In this vital, asset-rich area, the risk of ignoring the potential consequences of inadequate enforcement is monumental . . . (p. 1).

*   *   *

The failure to adequately review plans opens the door for fraud and abuse. Weak or non-existent internal controls by the plans enable sponsors and employers to defraud the plans by understating their required contributions. Inadequate internal controls also enable plan assets to be disbursed to ineligible individuals. Inadequate examination of excessive administrative costs can result in situations where nearly half of a sponsor's contributions are siphoned off to "middlemen" or "consultants." . . . the failure to verify the existence of plan investments, assure the accuracy of current valuations, and their degree of risk can lead to plan failures (p. 2).

*   *   *

Reports prepared by IPAs (independent public accountants) are of questionable value in monitoring benefit plan compliance with the criminal provisions of Title I of ERISA and Title 18 of the U.S. Code. . . . As unfortunately has been demonstrated by the recent savings and loan crisis, government regulation of an industry does not assure that invested assets are protected. Limited scope reviews, under ERISA, although classified as audits, do not adequately test the employee benefit plan assets. These limited scope audits also result in reports with disclaimed opinions and limited liability for the auditors. They are of little value and give no assurance of asset integrity to benefit plan participants (p. 1).

*   *   *

In a situation with a striking number of parallels, a recently issued GAO report sharply criticized the public accounting profession for its failure to identify and report on significant problems in the management and operation of the savings and loan (S&L) industry. . . .

An unknown portion of the $1.6 trillion in assets that are currently in private pension plans likewise may be at risk, for many of those same reasons. . . . Because of the absence of DOL monitoring and IPA reporting, the OIG is concerned about the degree to which employee benefit plans may be at risk to fraudulent schemes (p. 3).

* * *

I am concerned about the effectiveness of the Department's enforcement of law designed to protect the pension and benefit plans (p. i).

Case Example Excerpts

On March 17, 1989, five former officials and associates of Lundberg Industries, Ltd. (LIL), a New Mexico corporation, were indicted by a Federal grand jury in Albuquerque, N.M., for mail fraud, embezzlement, aiding and abetting, and conspiring to embezzle over $9 million in pension funds. The defendants were charged with stealing the retirement funds of over 900 active and retired employees of LIL. Named in the indictment were: Thomas D. Lundberg, president of LIL; John Sanders, an attorney; Samuel A. Longo, a financial consultant; Clarence David Donaldson, an insurance agent; and David Joel Boatright, an actuary and pension fund consultant. . . .

In furtherance of the alleged conspiracy, the investigation documented one scheme wherein Lundberg and Sanders, in December 1985, executed documents to purchase Potash Company of America for $3 million. With this purchase, LIL acquired three existing employee benefit plans with assets in excess of $11 million. With the assistance of Donaldson and Boatright, Lundberg and Sanders then obtained fictitious loans totaling over $2.5 million from one pension plan. The defendants converted the money to their own use.

In another scheme, it is alleged that Lundberg, Longo, and others not charged in the indictment, again aided by Boatright and Donaldson, conspired, through a complicated real estate transaction involving the purchase of 127 acres of undeveloped land in Texas, to authorize two more loans totaling $1,550,000 from the pension plans. The four defendants again converted the money to their own use (pp. 16–17).

* * *

David Friedland, who pled guilty in September 1988 to racketeering conspiracy involving the Mid-Jersey Trucking-Teamsters Local 701 Pension Fund . . . was the principal defendant in the case involving the fraudulent investment of over $20 million of the fund's money by the Omni Funding Group of Fort Lauderdale, Florida (p. 30).

CUSTODIAL FRAUD

*   *   *

In the Southern District of Florida, Alan F. Meyer, a Fort Lauderdale attorney and certified public accountant, was indicted. . . . According to the indictment, Meyer received a $1,075,000 loan from Omni Florida and used the money to buy out his partners' interest in a citrus grove. He then quitclaimed the grove title to Joseph Higgins, owner of Omni, for use as a tax shelter. Higgins was prohibited by law from obtaining personal benefit from the fund . . . [but] aided by Meyers Higgins was able to conceal his involvement (p. 30).

Note: It is hoped that the foregoing selected excerpts from the Inspector General's reports convey the sense of significant peril building in the areas indicated. If anyone reading this has any responsibility at all in the areas indicated (pension funds, for example), we recommend that you obtain the DOL semi-annual reports to the congress for periods beginning in 1988. Address your requests to:

U.S. Department of Labor
Office of Inspector General
Washington, DC 20210

GLOSSARY

Actual fraud: A fraud with actual intent to deceive. (Websters)

Affidavit: A statement taken with the declarant order oath. Also known as a "sworn statement."

Auditor (layman's conception): A man past middle age, spare, wrinkled, intelligent, cold, passive, noncommittal, with eyes like a codfish, polite in contact, but at the same time unresponsive, calm and damnably composed as a concrete post or plaster of Paris cast; a human petrification with a heart of feldspar and without the charm of the friendly germ, minus bowels, passion, or a sense of humor. Happily they never reproduce and all of them finally go to Hell. (Elbert Hubbard, *The CPA and His Profession*, American Institute of Accountants, 1954)

Best evidence: As between a supposed literal copy and the original, the copy is always liable to errors on the part of the copyist, whether by willfulness or by inadvertence; this contingency wholly disappears when the original is produced. Moreover, the original may contain, and the copy will lack, such features of handwriting, paper, and the like, as may afford the opponent valuable means of learning legitimate objections to the significance of the document. As between oral testimony, based on recollection, and the original, the added risk, almost the certainty, exists, of errors or recollection due to the difficulty of carrying in the memory literally the tenor of the document. (I.V. Wigmore, John Henry, *Evidence*, 4th ed., p. 1179, Boston Little Brown, 1988)

GLOSSARY

Business records act: A record of an act, condition, or event shall, insofar as relevant, be competent evidence if the custodian or other qualified witness testifies to its identity and the modes of its preparation and if it was made in the regular course of business, at or near the time of the act, condition, or event, and if, in the opinion of the court, the sources of information, method and time of preparation were such as to justify its admission. The underlying rationale permitting this exception to the hearsay rule is that business records have the earmark of reliability or probability of trustworthiness since they reflect the day-to-day operations of the enterprise and are relied upon in the conduct of business.

Burden of proof: The obligation of a party to meet the requirements of a rule of law that a fact be proved either by a preponderance of the evidence, or by a clear and convincing evidence, or beyond a reasonable doubt, as the case may be.

Case assessment: The consideration of the threats, risks, and vulnerabilities of a possible or known crime to establish the investigative parameters and help direct the investigative effort.

Circumstantial evidence: Evidence that is indirect and relies on inference evidence that a fact is more probably true than not true.

Clear and convincing evidence: That measure or degree of proof which will produce in the mind of the trier of facts a firm belief or conviction as to the facts sought to be established. Beyond preponderance but to the extent of certainty beyond a reasonable doubt as is required in criminal cases. For example, to rescind a contract on grounds that it was procured by fraudulent representations it must be proved that (1) there were actual or implied false representations of material matters of fact; (2) such representations were false; (3) such representations were made by one party to the other with knowledge of their falsity; (4) they were made with intent to mislead a party to rely thereon; (5) such party relied on such representations with a right to rely thereon.

Computer crimes: Any criminal scheme involving the intentional and direct use of computer equipment and/or related software.

Competency: The requirement of competency involves evidence offered that on its face is material and relevant and does not violate any exclusionary rule of evidence.

GLOSSARY

Contemporaneous notes: Notes made by an investigator and taken in an investigation which concerns acts or statements at the time those statements or acts are occurring.

Constructive fraud: In law, a fraud that is involved in an act or contract, which has a tendency to deceive or mislead other persons, to violate public or private confidence, or to impair or injure the public interests.

Corroborating evidence: Evidence supplementary to that already given, and tending to strengthen or confirm it. Additional evidence of a different character but to the same point.

Crime: An act committed in violation of a law prohibiting it, or committed in violation of a law ordering it.

Cumulative evidence: Evidence that goes to prove what has already been established by other evidence.

Declarant: The person making a statement.

Direct evidence: Testimony or real evidence which speaks directly to a material issue in a case without any cause to introduce references.

Documentary evidence: This evidence in the case of business records is authenticated by proof that shows a particular document is what the proponent claims it to be on its face.

Evidence: Means employed for the purpose of proving an unknown or disputed fact, and is either judicial or extrajudicial.

Fraud: An intentional perversion of the truth to induce another to part with some valuable thing belonging to him, or to surrender a legal right.

Fraud off-the-books: Fraud that does not involve the accounting records or underlying documentation.

Fraud on-the-books: Fraud that involves accounting records, and which can be theoretically detected through an examination of the accounting records or underlying documentation.

Hearsay: An out-of-court statement offered to prove the truth of what is asserted in an in-court statement. The general rule is that courts will not receive testimony of a witness as to what some other person told him as evidence of the existence of the fact asserted. For example, a bus company employee's testimony that he had received an oral report that two suitcases had been stolen and the thief apprehended is inadmissible hearsay in prosecution for the theft of suitcases. (*Rive v. U.S.*, 411 F.(2d) 485 (8th Cir 1969). Testimony is not hearsay when it is to prove only that a statement was made, and not the truth of the statement. Some authorities assert that former testimony is actually not hearsay, since it was under oath and subject to cross-examination. Others, however, recognize reported testimony as hearsay but recognize that it is admissible under an exception to the hearsay rule. Under either approach, when a witness for the prosecution or defendant is unavailable and cannot be produced at the present trial, the testimony of such a witness at a former criminal proceeding relating to the same subject matter and between the same parties will usually be admitted.

IFB: Invitation for Bid. A formal request issued to parties interested in submitting an offer to enter into a contract for goods or services. Commonly used by governmental entities.

Indicia (of fraud): Any evidence or indication, no matter how slight or inconclusive, that a crime has or may have occurred.

Interviewee: The person being interviewed.

Interviewer: The person conducting the interview and asking the questions.

Investigative plan: A method of organizing the efficient use of investigative resources to investigate a possible or known criminal act by assessing the crime, materials need, and immediately available facts.

Judicial notice of facts: Taken as true without the offering of evidence by the party who ordinarily should do so.

Jurat: That portion of the authenticating entry by the oath-giving official which shows that the statement was taken, sworn, or subscribed before the official, and the date and place of such action.

Legal evidence: Any species of proof, or probative matter, legally presented at the trial of an issue, by the act of the parties and through the medium of witness, records, documents, concrete objects, etc., for the purpose of inducing belief in the minds of the court or jury as to their contention. Legal evidence is that which is used or is intended to be used at a trial or at inquiries before courts, judges, commissioners, referees, etc. That which demonstrates or makes clear or ascertains the truth of the very fact or point in issue, either on the one side or the other.

Malfeasance: Evil and wrongdoing or misconduct, especially in handling public affairs; as, an official who takes graft or otherwise violates his trust . . . the doing of an act which a person ought not to do; an illegal deed;—often used of official misconduct. A malfeasant is a criminal.

Materiality: Materiality exists when the evidence offered relates to one or more of the substantive legal issues involved in the case.

Misconduct: Dishonest or bad management, especially by persons entrusted or engaged to act on another's behalf.

Misfeasance: In law—wrongdoing; specifically, the doing of a lawful act in an unlawful manner, so that there is an infringement on the rights of another or others; distinguished from *malfeasance* and *nonfeasance*.

Negligence: In law—failure to exercise the care that the circumstances justly demand; omission of duty in doing or forbearing; an act or instance of negligence or carelessness.

Nonfeasance: A failure to perform a duty. Omission to do something, especially what ought to have been done.

Preponderance of the evidence: Refers to the quality of the evidence, that is, its convincing quality, the weight and the effect that it has on the jurors' minds. Rests with the plaintiff.

Presumptions of fact: If Fact A is proved then Fact B may be concluded. Sometimes are called *inferences* (permissive).

Presumptions of law: A substitute for evidence. If a party proves in court that Fact A is true then Fact B must also be true without further proof. The judge is honest, the records of any court have been kept accurately, the accused in a criminal case is innocent, all witnesses are sane and sober, and that if a person is found dead he has not been murdered (mandatory).

Proactive: A term used to describe the general work habits of an auditor. That is, in the realm of fraud, to search for evidence of fraud even though none has been observed.

Proof: Effect of evidence, it is the establishment of fact by evidence. Evidence is the medium of proof, proof is the effect of evidence.

Proof is the conviction or persuasion of the mind of a judge or a jury, by the exhibition of evidence, of the reality of a fact alleged.

Prima facie evidence: If unexplained or uncontradicted is sufficient to carry a case to the jury and to sustain a verdict in favor of the issue which it supports but which may be contradicted by other evidence.

Reactive: A term used to describe the general work habits of a criminal investigator. That is, to search for evidence of fraud, after fraud is suspected.

Real evidence: Physical evidence perceptible to the senses. Evidence furnished by things themselves, on view or inspection, as distinguished from the description of them by the mouth of the witness.

Reasonable doubt: It is not a mere possible doubt, because everything relating to human affairs, and depending on moral evidence, is open to some possible or imaginary doubt. It is the state of the case, which, after the entire comparison and consideration of all the evidence, leaves the minds of jurors in that condition that they cannot say they feel an abiding conviction, to a moral certainty, of the truth of the charge. The degree of probability must depend on the mind of the reasonable and just man who is considering the particular subject matter.

Relevancy: Relevancy is a question of probativeness. Does the evidence tend to make the material issue more probably true or untrue? If so, it could be construed to be relevant.

RFP: Request for Proposal. See *IFB: Invitation for Bid*.

Search and seizure: Evidence is admissible if it is (1) obtained under a properly issued and executed search warrant; (2) obtained incidental to a lawful arrest following the rules as to the scope of the search (*Chimel v. California*, 395 US 752 23 L.Ed. (2d) 685, 89 S.Ct. 2034 (1969)); (3) obtained after a proper waiver of the constitutional rights; (4) obtained from a vehicle which is moving or about to be moved when proper conditions exist (*Carroll v. U.S.*, 267 US 132 69 L.Ed. 543, 45 S.Ct. 280 (1925)); or (5) seized from an area not protected by the Constitution (*Katz v. U.S.*, 389 US 347, 19 L.Ed. (2d) 576, 88 S.Ct. 507 (1967)). Also, evidence is generally considered admissible if obtained by a private individual who has no connection with an enforcement official, as the constitutional provisions are interpreted to protect one against official action and not private action. And evidence is admissible even though the constitutional protection is violated if the person has no right to challenge the search. Not only is the evidence obtained by an illegal search or a search in violation of the Constitution inadmissible, any information obtained as a result of the illegal act is generally excluded (Fruit of the Poisonous Tree Doctrine).

Stipulation: Substitute for evidence. A concession by both parties to the existence or nonexistence of a fact, to the contents of a document, or to the testimony of a witness.

Sufficiency of evidence: In determining the sufficiency of the evidence to sustain a conviction, the question is not whether evidence forecloses all possibility of doubt but whether the evidence, construed most favorably for the prosecution, is such that a jury might find the defendant guilty beyond a reasonable doubt.

Testimony: Evidence that comes to the court through witnesses speaking under oath or affirmation.

White-collar crime (1): Nonviolent criminal acts, which involve the use of deceit, trickery, concealment, dishonesty, or embezzlement for the purpose of obtaining personal gains.

White-collar crime (2): A crime, such as fraud, embezzlement, etc., committed by a person in business, government, or a profession in the course of his or her "occupational activities."

Wiretapping and eavesdropping: *Katz v. U.S.* 389 US 347(1967) rejected the contention that surveillance without trespass and without the seizure of material fell outside the purview of the Constitution. It is clear that wiretapping and eavesdropping are within the protection of the Fourth Amendment.

BIBLIOGRAPHY

American Institute of Certified Public Accountants. *Audit and Accounting Manual.* New York: American Institute of Certified Public Accountants, 1990.

Aylesworth, George N., and Marianne Swan. "Telecommunications Fraud Devices". *FBI Law Enforcement Bulletin* (March 1986): 1–4.

Bar Bri. *Evidence.* New York: Harcourt Brace Jovanovich Legal and Professional Publications, 1984.

Beekman, Mary Ellen. "Automobile Insurance Fraud Pays . . . and Pays Well." *FBI Law Enforcement Bulletin* (March 1986): 17–21.

Chimel vs. California, 395 US 752 (1968).

Cookingham, Vincent P. "Organized Crime: The Corporation as Victim." *Security Management* (July 1985) : 28–31.

Dee, Joseph M. "White Collar Crime: A Tie That Binds." *Security Management* (January 1985): 18–22.

Denes, Richard F. "Commercial Bribery: The White Collar Crime of the '80s." *Security Management* (April 1985): 56–62.

Hurley, John E. "Cargo Documentation Fraud." *Security Management* (February 1983): 39–40.

Inbau, Fred E., John E. Reid, and Joseph F. Buckley. *Criminal Interrogation and Confessions.* Baltimore: Williams & Wilkins, 1986.

Jensen, D. Lowell. "Who Pays the Price of White Collar Crime?" *Security Management.* Part 1 (September 1986): 141–148; Part 2 (October 1986): 87–92.

Katz vs. U.S., 389 US 347 (1967).

Kleberg, John R., and C. Allen Shaffer. "Evidence Exhibits in White Collar Crime Cases." *FBI Law Enforcement Bulletin* (July 1981): 1–6.

BIBLIOGRAPHY

Legal Lines. *Criminal Law.* 4th ed. Gardena, Calif.: Law Distributors, 1976.

Legal Lines. *Criminal Procedure.* 6th and 8th eds. Gardena, Calif.: Law Distributors, 1972; 1980.

McChesney, Kathleen L. "Operation Defcon: A Multiagency Approach to Defense Fraud Investigations." *FBI Law Enforcement Bulletin* (March 1988): 16–19.

North vs. U.S., USSC (1989). 264 US appelate 265 (1989) 829 Fed 2d50 (1987).

Orsagh, Thomas. "White Collar Informers: Getting Your Money's Worth." *Security Management* (October 1986): 39–43.

Osborn vs. U.S., USSC (1966). 395 US 752 (1968).

Pizzo, Stephen, *Inside Job: The Looting of America's Savings and Loans/* Stephen Pizzo, Mary Fricker, Paul Muolo, 1989, McGraw-Hill Publishing Company.

Raffel, Robert T. "Airline Ticket Fraud." *FBI Law Enforcement Bulletin* (December 1985): 1–4.

Seger, Karl A., and David J. Icove. "Power Theft: The Silent Crime." *FBI Law Enforcement Bulletin* (March 1988): 20–25.

Seleno, Jim. "Check Print." *FBI Law Enforcement Bulletin* (February 1989): 14–17.

Thornburgh, Richard L. "Characteristics of White Collar Crime." *Illinois Police Officer* (Summer 1977): 29–33.

U.S. Department of the Army. *Intelligence Interrogations.* Field Manual 30-15. Washington, D.C.: March 1969.

U.S. Department of Justice. *Prevention and Detection of Fraud, Waste and Abuse of Public Funds.* Special National Workshop. Washington, DC: Law Enforcement Assistance Administration, November 1979.

U.S. Department of Labor, Office of Inspector General, *Semiannual Report, October 1, 1988–March 31, 1989,* U.S. Government Printing Office.

U.S. Department of Labor, Office of Inspector General, *Semiannual Report, April 1, 1989–September 30, 1989,* U.S. Government Printing Office.

BIBLIOGRAPHY

U.S. Department of Labor, Office of Inspector General, *Semiannual Report, April 1, 1990–September 30, 1990,* U.S. Government Printing Office.

U.S. Department of Labor, Office of Inspector General, *Semiannual Report, October 1, 1989–March 31, 1990* U.S. Government Printing Office.

U.S. Department of Labor, Office of Inspector General, *Semiannual Report, October 1, 1990–March 31, 1991,* U.S. Government Printing Office.

U.S. Department of Treasury. *Interviewing.* [Text 36]. Glynco, Ga.: Federal Law Enforcement Training Center, October 1978.

U.S. Department of the Treasury. *Interviewing Part II (Note-taking/ Statement-taking).* [Text 36]. Glynco, Ga.: General Law Enforcement Training Center, March 1979.

Villano, Clair E. *Complaint and Referral Handling.* Operational Guide to White-Collar Crime Enforcement. Washington, D.C.: U.S. Department of Justice/Law Enforcement Assistance Administration, May 1980. (One of several guides on white-collar crime matters published in 1979–1980 by LEAA pursuant to Grant Number 77-TA-99-0008 granted to Batelle Memorial Institute Law and Justice Study Center. All guides are valuable.)

Wolf, Marshall L., and John Bree. "Blue Monday at the Bank." *Security Management* (May 1986): 49–52.

INDEX

INDEX

INDEX